Icebreakers
à la Carte

Icebreakers
à la Carte

Sandy Christian, MSW

Nancy Loving Tubesing, EdD

WHOLE PERSON ASSOCIATES
Duluth, Minnesota

Printed in the United States of America

10   9   8   7   6   5   4   3   2   1

WHOLE PERSON ASSOCIATES
210 W Michigan
Duluth, MN 55802-1908

CONTENTS

©1998 Whole Person Associates 210 W Michigan Duluth MN 55802   (800) 247-6789

©1998 Whole Person Associates 210 W Michigan Duluth MN 55802   (800) 247-6789

COMPLEMENTS & CONDIMENTS

DESSERT

Welcome to Icebreakers á la Carte

Whenever people gather for learning experiences, they usually benefit from simple structures that stimulate interaction and bring key points of the content to life. Icebreakers can accomplish both these goals at the same time—while they simultaneously generate group energy and synergy.

So, welcome to the **Icebreakers á la Carte** café, where the menu is sprinkled with creative choices for spicing up your group, training program, workshop, or class. Whatever your personal tastes and style, you'll find plenty of choices that fit your participants, setting, and subject matter. Feel free to pick and choose from the á la carte menu, mixing and matching icebreakers throughout your presentation or group process, to create a satisfying feast.

To whet your appetite and get in the mood, savor the **Ten Principles for Using Group Icebreakers** (page 13). Then plunge right into the feast.

The Icebreakers á la Carte Menu

In the **Appetizers** course, you will find icebreakers that work especially well in the beginning of a learning experience or at the start of each meeting of a multisession course or group. Most are brief (5–15 minutes).

Introductions (page 2) includes 25 innovative processes for getting acquainted.

Learning Names (page 23) offers 7 unusual ways to help participants learn one another's names—and a bit more.

Getting Issues on the Table (page 31) features 22 icebreakers that help set the tone and agenda for a session while evoking personal reflection and commitment and promoting group interaction.

The **Main Course** offers more substantial icebreakers that may introduce significant content for reflection and discussion. These processes take a bit more time, depending on the size of discussion groups (10–30 minutes).

Group Building Processes (page 55) offers 15 techniques for building a sense of commitment to the learning community and the agenda.

Conversation Starters (page 77) includes 23 handy icebreakers to help get the ball rolling anytime during the session. These open-framework processes are easy to adapt to your content and the background of your group.

Tools for Self-Awareness (page 91) explores the use of self-assessments as icebreakers and provides 10 ready-to-go instruments for group use.

Discussions & Brainstorming (page 107) presents a rationale for involving the entire group in peer learning, along with 11 structured exercises for promoting interaction and creative problem solving.

Analogies & Metaphors (page 117) provides 19 intriguing icebreakers that employ nonlinear thinking and paradigm shifts to gain new perspectives on the issues, self, and others.

Creative Activities (page 133) will tap into the enlivening creative energies of the group. Use these 17 offbeat icebreakers to engage different learning styles, provoke problem-solving, and promote group bonding.

Dip into the **Complements & Condiments** course when the group needs a quick change of pace or charge of vitality.

Zesty Interludes (page 152) provides 8 different icebreakers that will shift the mood and provide a refreshing break from content bombardment.

Sauces & Seasonings (page 161) celebrates the importance of sprinkling humor and playfulness into any learning experience and points to energizing rituals and activities scattered throughout **Icebreakers á la Carte.**

For **Dessert** we offer icebreakers that bring closure to the learning experience.

Farewells & Resolutions (page 168) includes 15 processes that help participants articulate their learnings and resolutions and bid farewell to their cohorts.

Guide to the Icebreakers á la Carte Courses

Each course section begins with an outline of **Group Dynamics Principles** that apply to using that style of icebreaker in your learning experience. Look here for the underlying rationale that makes icebreakers work well—or not so well—in this phase of group development.

In **Tips for Planning and Implementation,** you'll find strategies for choosing icebreakers, as well as helpful hints for effective leadership and special considerations for different kinds of groups.

The **Cautions** of each course section offer guidance from folks in the field who have learned the hard way about unexpected consequences of using icebreakers in groups. Look here for helpful hints in choosing appropriate icebreakers and being alert for potential hazards.

The actual icebreakers in each section begin with a **Key Icebreaker**, which is presented in expanded, step-by-step format. Use this sample as a model for fleshing out the many icebreakers that follow in the **à la carte** portion. These are in abbreviated format, outlining the materials needed and brief descriptions of the processes. Some icebreakers require **Worksheets**, which are included at the end of the section.

Welcome to our Table

We've spent over sixty years of our professional lives working with groups of all sizes and agendas, ranging from community education to group therapy to staff development to workshops and large conferences. We've taught social workers, psychologists, physicians, adult educators, corporate trainers, clergy, teachers, health care providers, and counselors. We've experimented with icebreakers in all kinds of settings and situations, many times creating them on the spot from the dynamics of the group and the inspiration of the moment. We've learned from the bombs as well as the strokes of genius.

We believe in icebreakers and invite you to sample from our collected wisdom. We also encourage you to trust your own wisdom. Modify, adapt, transform at will. Practice creating your own icebreakers from the resources around you—news tidbits, Internet humor, movies, self-

©1998 Whole Person Associates 210 W Michigan Duluth MN 55802   (800) 247-6789

help checklists, magazine features, metaphors from your life experiences, a comprehensive thesaurus. Be adventurous and courageous. Learn from your creations, both the magical moments and the less than magical ones. Above all, have fun! Your enthusiasm will be contagious.

Bon appetit!

Sandy Stewart Christian, MSW
Missoula, Montana

Nancy Loving Tubesing, EdD
Placitas, New Mexico

TEN PRINCIPLES FOR USING ICEBREAKERS

All groups need icebreakers. The world is full of shy people who need focus and a very specific way to talk frankly about themselves. Icebreakers provide a vehicle for sharing select personal information, freeing people from constraining anxiety, and guiding participants into authentic, purposeful, often touching conversations.

Icebreakers are not just for getting acquainted. They are especially useful for groups of strangers; but even well-acquainted groups can use icebreakers to ease into a course or group discussion, provide focus for group activities, and establish the proper climate for learning. From first meetings to final farewells, icebreakers pave the way for people to be real.

Icebreakers make the group, and its members, attractive to participants. Not everyone will like everyone else in a group, but the more people are attracted to other participants, and discover common interests, goals, and values, the more eager they will be to participate. Icebreakers induce people to share in spontaneous ways that stimulate lively interaction and draw people to one another.

Icebreakers affirm the rights of participants. Everyone who joins a group has human rights: to be recognized as individual, to have input into some group decisions, to have an equal opportunity to participate in the group, to establish goals and work towards them, to have others respect personal privacy, and to have the group be a safe, secure place in which no one is belittled or degraded. Icebreakers direct participants into activities and behaviors that uphold and affirm these rights in words and actions.

Icebreakers should be relevant to all participants. Everything you do should be relevant to the culture of the group, and its members; icebreakers as well as other group activities should be presented in the context of participants' life experience and be relevant in language, values, and style.

Trust is the most important variable to consider when using icebreakers. Icebreakers help establish trust and contribute to its strength throughout the life of the group. The bottom line is, "Can I be honest here and say what I really think and feel?" If the answer is no, the group is constrained from lively, spontaneous communication and deterred in its purpose. Icebreakers remind people, over and over, that open, heart-searching communication is like a wind blowing the group spirit in the right direction.

Icebreakers are vehicles for shaping open group systems. The best environment for learning is an open system, one that accepts and welcomes diverse people, invites honest communication, expresses warmth and affection freely, challenges individuals to grow, shares power with all its members, provides support for people who need it, respects personal boundaries, and honors the limits of the group itself.

Icebreakers provide a way of quickly introducing these values to the group in action and words. Since the rules of the system are often decided in the first few minutes of interaction (without ever talking about them, just by watching each other and the group leader for clues about how to behave), it's all the more important that icebreakers be used early on to lay the foundation for an open system.

Equal, active participation is an implicit goal of all icebreakers. Successful groups are the responsibility of all participants. The more you inform people about their choices, the more they can take responsibility for group learning. Knowing what the leader has planned, why a particular activity was chosen, and what their roles and responsibilities will be, helps group members make clear decisions about how they want to participate.

 Most groups need a balance of activities. Too much of any one thing creates a lop-sided group; overly friendly, chatty groups may never get down to business, while "all work and no play" groups may suffer from boredom. Most groups function best with a mixture of activities, some light-hearted, others serious.

Experiential, holistic learning is ideal. Learning involves the whole person: mind, body, spirit, relationships, and emotions. When group activities incorporate all these aspects of learning and accomodate the different learning styles of individuals, the chances are great that group members will have a complete experience, one they can integrate with previous experience and apply to everyday life, resulting in a genuine change of attitudes, perceptions, feelings, thoughts, and behaviors.

APPETIZERS

Introductions

Learning Names

Getting Issues on the Table

INTRODUCTIONS

Introductions are social rituals that allow strangers to become acquainted with one another and with the group itself. As people learn to know one another, they are also initiated into the group process, receiving a taste of the group as a system, with its unique culture, values, and rules.

GROUP DYNAMICS PRINCIPLES

The first stage of group development is getting acquainted. In large groups, personal introductions may not be needed or practical, but in small groups they are essential. If people are going to work (or play) closely together, they need to know and be known by other group members. Getting acquainted is the first step toward building trust, cohesion, and commitment.

During introductions, people have the opportunity to test the water. Do participants share similar values, interests, and goals? Will each individual be accepted and respected? Will the group be friendly and welcoming? If early experiences with introductions are positive, participants will relax, feel comfortable, and be willing to risk greater involvement with the group.

Introductions create lasting impressions of the group. First impressions persist throughout the life-span of the group, so it is important that people have the opportunity to experience one another in a balanced manner. This means that during introductions, everyone is treated equally with respect to time, attention, respect, and welcome. No one individual or subgroup is allowed to dominate or receive special treatment; status and power differences are leveled by a uniform introductory process. When fairness is the way it's done, people remember it.

Any time new group members are added, introductions are needed. This is what keeps the power balanced. Introductions create doorways into the group; without this initiation, newcomers are not admitted through the door and remain outsiders, less powerful than insiders. Introductions alone cannot keep the power balanced, but they are important factors in maintaining an open group, one that allows for new members, new ideas, and new learning.

TIPS FOR PLANNING AND IMPLEMENTATION

Use group size, purpose, and time limits as a guide. Introductions may not be practical or appropriate for large groups, especially if people want or expect anonymity or if time is limited. But for most groups, introductions are expected and enjoyed. Even quick introductions to neighbors will loosen people up and add personal warmth to the group experience.

Introductions work best in pairs or small groups. Individual introductions in groups larger than eight to ten people are a waste of time: it takes too long, is repetitive, hard to hear, and almost impossible to remember, so people become bored, tired, impatient, or frustrated with the process. It's more interesting to do introductions in pairs, trios, or small groups of four to six people, followed by some method of reconnecting with the large group. Pairs can introduce partners; small groups can share selected information with the large group.

Structure time limits for introductions. Keep things moving along by designating time limits for sharing (one to two minutes each). Keep time and signal when to stop, rotate speakers, or switch partners. In large groups, try a bell, funky whistle, or harmonica as a friendly signal. Small groups can appoint a timekeeper or rotate this responsibility among group members. The trick is to keep it brief, lively, and interesting.

Make introductions a positive experience. Asking participants to introduce themselves by talking about positive traits, abilities, attitudes, or experiences is a great way to get started. You build on past success and reinforce feelings of pride, competency, and self-esteem. You also send a clear message that everyone has strengths and can make a valuable contribution to the group.

Invite participants to talk about past group experiences. If you can include questions about previous group experiences with introductions, do so. It will shed light on each person's present attitude toward group participation and provide a safe vehicle for discussing individual concerns at the beginning of the group when ground rules are normally clarified and negotiated.

CAUTIONS

Check out group members' desire for anonymity. If you are not sure, poll the group. Groups can be very intimate without ever sharing names or other demographic data. If members wish to remain anonymous, make sure there is an overt agreement to keep personal identity confidential. Even if people don't tell their names, it is not uncommon for someone in the group to recognize someone else, so this insistence on anonymity, while it may seem picky to some, is reassuring to others.

Prevent inappropriate self-disclosure during introductions. Most inappropriate disclosures can be prevented by selecting low-risk introduction exercises, combining them with clear guidelines about what information to share and how much time each person has to share. Be firm about time limits; it's not fair to anyone to let one person control the process.

Respect the group's response to introductions. If the group does not like the questions or activities, there may be a good reason. Let the group give input about this and listen to their concerns. Be flexible and try a different approach if necessary.

1 MY OBITUARY

By writing their own obituary and using it for introductions, participants share values, dreams, and lifetime goals.

Goals

To get acquainted.

To clarify personal values and goals.

Time

15 minutes

Materials

Worksheet: *My Obituary* (page 16)

Process

1. Tell the group that you have an intriguing, unusual way for participants to get acquainted: by writing their own obituary.

   ☞ *The idea of writing a personal obituary is bound to make some people uneasy, so expect some groans and moans. Be reassuring and confident about the value of this exercise.*

2. Hand out *My Obituary* worksheets and give instructions for personal reflections about life goals, values, and purpose.

   ▪ Think about your ideal life, the kind of life you would have if you lived your life and dreams to the fullest: where you would live (and die), how long would you live, what your field of work would be, other special accomplishments or things you would be remembered for, the value of your estate, and the engraving on your tombstone.

   ▪ You have five minutes to write your own obituary.

      ☞ *Signal when four minutes have passed and then again when five minutes have passed and time is up.*

3. Divide the large group into small groups of four to six people and give guidelines for introductions.

   ▪ Join a small group and sit in a circle facing each other.

   Beginning with the person who lived to be the oldest on

their written obituary, introduce yourself by reading your
obituary aloud to the group.

▪ When you have finished reading your obituary, you may
add a few comments, if you wish, to further explain what
you have written or respond to questions others may have.

▪ Each person has two minutes to share. The person to the
left of the speaker will keep time.

4. When everyone has read their obituary and responded to
questions about it, invite participants to share reactions to this
exercise.

▪ Discuss your responses to this exercise. Describe your feelings about writing your obituary and reading it aloud.

5. After two or three minutes, interrupt the discussions and
invite participants to share responses with the entire group.
Solicit reactions from each small group, making sure that
each group is heard from. Summarize common experiences
and then reconvene the large group and move on to the next
activity.

INTRODUCTIONS À LA CARTE

2 UNFORGETTABLE

1. Ask participants to introduce themselves to someone they don't know well. Partners should tell each other something unforgettable about themselves.

2. Repeat with several different partners.

3. If small groups are needed for the next activity, after the final exchange, ask pairs to pair up, forming quartets or sextets. Each person can then introduce his "unforgettable" partner.

3 UNBELIEVABLE ME

1. Instruct participants to find a partner and tell each other something about themselves that others would find fantastic or unbelievable. Encourage people to make up an outrageous quality or experience to share, if necessary.

2. After two minutes, signal people to find a new partner and repeat the process, this time sharing a different unbelievable, amazing thing about themselves.

3. Guide participants through three more repetitions of this process. Ask for examples of the unbelievable people in the group.

4 EXAGGERATION

1. Ask participants to find a partner and briefly exchange information on the circumstances and motivations that resulted in their presence here.

2. As conversation dies down, have people switch partners and retell their stories of how they came to be in this particular group, this time exaggerating the story, using exciting words and dramatic gestures to communicate.

3. Ask the group what they noticed about the effect of exaggeration on their mood and energy.

Variation: Use this dramatic technique to exaggerate and energize any type of introduction.

©2003 Whole Person Associates 210 W Michigan Duluth MN 55802   (800) 247-6789

5 FUN AND GAMES

1. Assign participants to a small group and have people introduce themselves as a game, telling why they picked a specific
   game. To stimulate creativity, give a few examples of board
   games (Monopoly, chess, Uncle Wiggly), kids' games (hop-
   scotch, tag, dodge ball), card games (poker, Old Maid,
   canasta), sports games (badminton, baseball, ultimate Fris-
   bee), word games (hangman, fictionary).

2. For the next scheduled activity, regroup participants by the
   type of game people chose for introductions.

6 PLEASING PERSONALITY

1. Tell everyone to pair up with someone and share what they
   think are their most pleasing personality traits.

2. Instruct each pair to join another pair and then introduce their
   partners by telling about one of their partner's most pleasing
   personality traits.

3. Ask each foursome to join another foursome and again
   introduce their partners by telling about a different pleasing
   personality trait.

7 CELEBRITY CONNECTIONS

1. Ask participants to think of remote connections they have to
   famous people. These can be extreme or ridiculous, such as
   "I picked a lilac off a bush on the street where Ben Afleck
   lives," or "My cousin delivered mail to the neighbor of Barry
   Bonds," or "I have the same middle name as Hilary Clinton."

2. Assign everyone to small groups of 8 people and invite
   participants to introduce themselves by telling their name,
   where they are from, and their celebrity connection.

3. Reconvene the group; ask participants to vote on the best
   celebrity connections; and give silly prizes to the winners.

8 WALK IN MY SHOES

1. Ask people to put one of their shoes in a pile in the center of

the room. Use these shoes to create small groups, putting four to six shoes at random in piles around the room.

2. Instruct participants to locate the pile including their shoe and join the others whose shoes were in the same pile to make introductions. After exchanging names, each group member chooses a shoe (not their own) from the pile and, holding the shoe in hand, tells how she imagines it might be to "walk in the shoes" of its owner. The holder of the smallest shoe in the group begins.

9 NUMBER PLEASE

Props: Decide in advance how many small groups you will want for introductions and then assign a number to each group. Make up sets of six to eight cards with that same number, and mix all number cards together in a basket or box.

1. As people arrive, tell them to pick a number and then find other participants with that number, sit down together, and learn each other's names.

2. Participants take turns telling about a significant number in their lives (e.g., blood pressure, lucky number, graduation year, birth date, years until retirement, license plate, number of children).

Variation: As people arrive, give them a sequential number to write on their name tag (e.g., 1–100 crossed off in order, preprinted tickets used for raffles, deli-counter pull-off numbers). Use these numbers to create new groups at different points in the session (e.g., all numbers ending in 6 together, all odd numbers together, all numbers ending in the teens and twenties together).

10 MYSTERY GUEST

1. Ask each person to write down something intriguing about himself on a card. Then collect the cards and read each one aloud, asking people to guess the "mystery guest" from the description.

2. If the group is larger than ten people, form smaller groups and let each group collect their cards and guess together.

11 LABELS

Props: Name tags or self-adhesive labels, markers

1. Give everyone a name tag or label and marker. Participants write their name and best and worst attributes on the label, put the label on, and silently walk around reading each other's labels.

2. After all have met nonverbally, ask people to choose a partner (or join in small groups), make verbal introductions, and give an example of when their attributes caused them difficulty or brought them satisfaction.

12 OPPOSITES ATTRACT

Props: Prior to the session, make a set of matching word-card pairs by printing a word on a three-by-five-inch index card and its opposite on another (e.g., hot and cold, Republican and Democrat, agony and ecstasy).

1. As participants come in, tell them to take a card and keep their word secret. At the appropriate time, announce that opposites attract and ask people to find the person who holds their matching (opposite meaning) card. Explain the ground rule: people must introduce themselves by name before asking to see another person's word card.

2. Partners get acquainted by telling how these words apply (or don't apply) to themselves.

13 HOURGLASS

Props: Small hourglasses (egg or game timers), one for each small group (four to six people).

1. Form small groups and invite participants to reflect on how they prefer to spend their leisure time. Ask which person from each group slept the latest that morning. Give late sleepers the hourglass.

2. Beginning with the late sleeper, each person takes a turn talking about their leisure activities. When the sand runs out, the timer is passed to the next person, who takes a turn, and so on around the group.

3. Ask people to tip the hour glass again, this time sharing something they love to do, but never seem to have time for.

14 BABY FACE

Props: Participants each bring a baby or childhood picture of themselves.

1. Display all baby pictures. After people have a chance to view the photo gallery, have participants guess the identities of each picture. (Hold them up one-by-one and ask the group for an ID or number the pictures and have people write their guesses or use small slips of paper for each person to ID each photo).
2. As each baby face is correctly identified, the corresponding adult describes what other people have told her she was like as a baby (or at the age of the picture).

15 MONKEY WRENCHES

Props: one monkey wrench for each small group

1. Hold up a monkey wrench and explain the common expression "throwing a monkey wrench into the works," which means adding something (like a complication) that doesn't fit with your needs or interferes with your process or plans.
2. Create small groups of 4–6 people. Give each group a monkey wrench and instruct participants to get acquainted by passing the wrench around the group, each taking 2 minutes to talk about times when there has been a monkey wrench in their life.

16 NAME-TIE COLLAGE

Props: three-by-five-inch index cards, markers, magazines, scissors, glue, paper punches, string or yarn precut in 36-inch lengths.

1. Invite participants to make a name-tie collage by writing their name on top of a card and embellishing it with graphics that represent their present health status or wellness goals (or other theme related to your content). People glue on appropriate pictures, words, or slogans from magazines.
2. Instruct participants to think about what they learned about

health (or your theme) from their parents or other significant adults. People write on their card one thing they learned about health (your theme) from Mom (or female role model) and one thing they learned about health (your theme) from Dad (or male role model).

3. Show participants how to make a bolo tie of their collage by punching holes in it and threading string through. When everyone has put on their name-ties, have participants walk around and talk to four different people about the theme. Signal every minute for switching partners.

Variation: Have people pair up with someone and make a poster, using images of wellness and images of disease (or your themes).

17 POST-IT

Props: small pad of Post-it notes for each participant

1. Distribute Post-it notes. Invite people to walk around and introduce themselves to as many people as they can in 5 minutes, exchanging some bit of information related to your theme, and jotting down each person's name on a Post-it note, along with a brief note that will help them remember that individual. Notes can be stuck on a sheet of paper for later reference.

2. Later in the session, ask several participants to introduce someone they met earlier, using their Post-it notes as memory ticklers.

Variation: In a workshop setting, challenge participants to make contact and conversation with each of their Post-it buddies during a break.

18 CARTOON

1. Give everyone a sheet of blank paper and instruct them to make a cartoon that they believe describes themselves. When all are finished, participants should pair up, show their cartoon, and tell about it.

2. After three or four minutes, ask pairs to join with two or three

other pairs, creating groups of six to eight people. Each person introduces their partner, and explains their partner's cartoon to the group.

19 YOU CAN QUOTE ME ON THAT

Handout: *You Can Quote Me On That* (page 17)

1. Distribute handouts and ask people to read through the quotations, proverbs, and maxims, marking any that especially spark their interest.
2. Divide participants into small groups for introductions. People take turns introducing themselves, using one of their marked quotations and telling why this particular quote touched them.

20 WHAT'S MY LINE?

Worksheet: list of the current occupations of all group members, with spaces for writing the corresponding names, prepared in advance and duplicated

1. Distribute worksheets and invite participants to walk around the group, getting acquainted by guessing the other person's occupation. Tell people to attempt several guesses before asking the person reveal her true occupation.
2. Participants sign the questioner's worksheet beside their current occupation when the correct one is revealed/discovered.

21 PULLING TEETH

Worksheet: *Pulling Teeth* (page 18)

1. Distribute worksheets and ask participants to reflect on their patterns of self disclosure, using the individual teeth on the worksheet to jot their responses to these two questions:
   - What topics, issues, or feelings are you unlikely to share in a group?
   - When will other group members feel like they are "pulling teeth" to get a response from you??
2. Form small groups. Invite participants to get acquainted by

describing their off-limits areas and then answering a question in one of these areas asked by the person to his or her right.

22 DAYS OF OUR LIVES

Worksheet: *Days of Our Lives* (page 19)

1. Distribute worksheets and ask participants to write about their daily lives, filling in the blanks with their first responses.
2. Create small groups. Ask people to introduce themselves in turn, reading their daily life story aloud to the group.

Variation: Ask participants to discuss what's missing or what changes they would like to make in their daily patterns.

23 BANNER YEAR

Worksheet: *Banner Year* (page 20)

1. Hand out worksheets and ask everyone to make a banner for the past year celebrating one or more special achievements they are proud of and want to proclaim to the world.
2. Form small groups. Participants introduce themselves, show their banner, and share the story of their banner year.

Variation: Ask participants to create a banner for the group or for a particular group session. Is there a major message they want to proclaim to the world about what they have learned?

24 SUPERSTAR

Worksheet: *Superstar* (page 21)

1. Hand out worksheets and ask participants to consider in what ways they are a superstar, writing an example of their star status in each point of the star.
2. Form small groups of four to six people. Participants introduce themselves, telling about the five ways they shine.
3. Solicit examples of star qualities from each group or have each person stand up and introduce herself, sharing one superstar quality.

25 YOU OUGHT TO BE IN PICTURES

Props: Polaroid camera and enough film to take a picture of each participant, glue or double-sided tape

Worksheet: *You Ought to Be in Pictures* (page 22)

1. Give each person an worksheet. Ask them to fill it out and fasten their photo on it, as they would on an ID form.

2. Post the ID forms around the room in a rogues' gallery. Invite participants to pair up with someone they do not know, tour the gallery together, read each other's ID forms, and exchange answers to the Ask Me questions.

MY OBITUARY

(Mr./Mrs./Ms.) _____, who resided at

(your dream address) _____ ,

was _____ years of age and had spent _____ years in the

field of _____ .

In addition, (Mr./Mrs./Ms.) _____ will be remembered for:

1. _____

2. _____

3. _____

4. _____

5. _____

6. _____

7. _____

8. _____

Authorities believe the estate will be nearly _____

and that a headstone engraved with ” _____

_____ ”

is specified in the will.

YOU CAN QUOTE ME ON THAT

A man's life is what his thoughts make it. (Marcus Aurelius)

If you cannot get rid of the family skeleton, you may as well make it dance. (G.B. Shaw)

Tell me what you brag about and I'll tell you what you lack. (Spanish proverb)

If you scatter thorns, don't go barefoot. (Italian proverb)

The best mirror is an old friend. (English proverb)

Love must be learned, and learned again and again; there is no end to it. Hate needs no instruction, but waits only to be provoked. (Katherine Ann Porter)

Notice the difference between what happens when a man says to himself, "I have failed three times," and what happens when he says, "I am a failure." (S.I. Hayakawa)

Work expands so as to fill the time available for its completion. (Parkinson's Law)

I've had a lot of trouble in my life, most of which never happened. (Mark Twain)

Remember, no one can make you feel inferior without your consent. (Eleanor Roosevelt)

Seven days without laughter makes one weak. (Joel Goodman)

You grow up the day you have your first real laugh—at yourself. (Ethyl Barrymore)

Many a true word is spoken in jest. (English proverb)

The best way out is always through. (Robert Frost)

Pick yourself up. Dust yourself off. Start all over again. (Dorothy Fields)

Most people are about as happy as they make up their minds to be. (Abraham Lincoln)

If at first you don't succeed, try, try again. Then quit. No use being a (darn) fool about it. (W.C. Fields)

The biggest disease today is not leprosy or tuberculosis, but rather the feeling of being unwanted, uncared for and deserted by everybody. (Mother Theresa)

The process of writing, any form of creativity, is a power intensifying life. (Rita Mae Brown)

I am visible—see this Indian face—yet I am invisible. I both blind them with my beak nose and am their blind spot. But I exist, we exist. They'd like to think I have melted in the pot. But I haven't, we haven't. (Gloria Anzaldua)

You cannot shake hands with a clenched fist. (Indira Gandhi)

PULLING TEETH

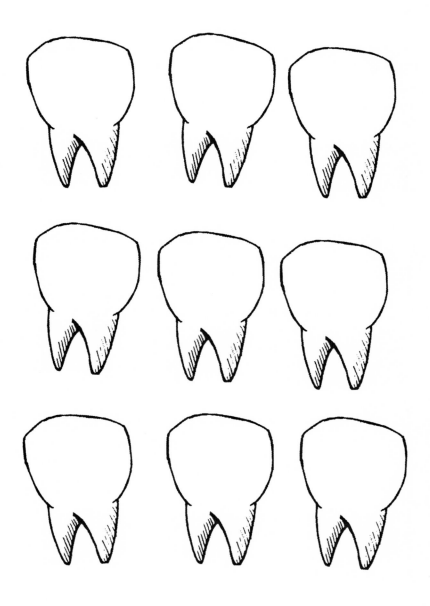

DAYS OF OUR LIVES

I get up and then . . . _____

and then . . . _____

and then . . . _____

and then I get these . . . _____

and then . . . _____

and then at lunch . . . _____

and then . . . _____

and then . . . _____

I go home . . . _____

and then . . . _____

and . . . _____

and . . . _____

and . . . _____

every . . . _____

and . . . _____

and . . . _____

bed . . . _____

and then . . . _____

BANNER YEAR

SUPER STAR

YOU OUGHT TO BE IN PICTURES

place photo here

Name _____

Best work skill _____

Unusual family history _____

My favorite meal or comfort food _____

Ask me about _____

LEARNING NAMES

The icebreakers in this section are designed to help participants learn each other's names and to personalize interaction between group members.

GROUP DYNAMICS PRINCIPLES

Names are important identity symbols, which serve as powerful connectors for people. Taking time to make these connections sets standards that everyone counts, each person's uniqueness is valued, and participation by all is important. Being known by name is the first step in belonging to a group.

Learning names reduces anxiety. Most people feel a twinge—if not a surge—of anxiety about participating in a new group, especially when there are no familiar faces in the room. Learning names is a basic, yet effective, way of putting people at ease.

Knowing names facilitates conversation. Trying to talk to other group members when you don't know their names is like trying to eat a meal without silverware: it's awkward and uncomfortable. Knowing names is a social lubricant that allows you to address others directly and personalize conversations.

Learning names sends a message. The message is that you care about participants. In the early stages of group formation, participants are seeking direct and indirect answers to questions about the group: What can be accomplished here? Will this group be relevant to my needs or goals? Will I be accepted? Attentive leaders who help others get acquainted send a powerful message about the value of listening and the worth of each person.

TIPS FOR PLANNING AND IMPLEMENTATION

Decide how important it is to learn names in your group. For ongoing groups or groups that are going to work together on a task, it is very important that all names are known by all team members, so that everyone is recognized and power is equally shared. In larger groups, it's good to have some small groups in which people can learn the names of others and find buddies to talk to during breaks. Decide how important learning names is for achieving your goals.

Consider the size of your group. In larger workshops, include other icebreakers to keep people moving and meeting others. The more people learn to know others, the greater the chances of stimulating energy and enthusiasm for creative learning.

Be a role model. If possible, get a list of participants' names in advance and practice remembering (and pronouncing) each person's name. Use names when you call on people. This rewards those who have risked speaking up in the group and reinforces memory of the name for other participants Don't forget to model assertive behavior: if you forget someone's name—ask! It's okay to make mistakes.

Develop a process for incorporating newcomers. Every time you add new members to an ongoing group, it's important to provide a process for the newcomers to learn the names of others in the group. This helps prevent power alliances or splits between insiders and outsiders. Everyone should be an insider.

Use name tags and other memory aids. Name tags should be written in large letters, readable at a distance, and appropriate for all types of clothing. The bolo tie style (worn around the neck), using three-by-five inch index cards hung with yarn or string, is a trustworthy choice: no sharp pins to poke holes in clothes or skin, no sticky glue to cling to fabric.

To enhance name memory in task-oriented groups, consider distributing handouts with participants' names before introductions and encourage people to make notes during introductions to help them remember each person. Participants may have their own memory tricks to share with the group.

CAUTIONS

Learning names can take a lot of time, especially in groups of more than eight people. Consider the group size, purpose, and time factors and plan accordingly.

Some people or groups prefer anonymity. Be sensitive to individual or group needs for anonymity or confidentiality. If you are not sure what people want, ask directly at the beginning of the workshop. Discuss issues and concerns and seek consensus among participants about ground rules or expectations.

Avoid resistance by matching activities to the group. Childish games may not go over well with a group of executives in a business setting, but they may be a big hit with adults engaged in a playful summer retreat. Highly anxious groups will only get more uptight if you ask them to perform activities that make them feel exposed. Don't set yourself up for resistance by being unprepared; take time before your first meeting to learn about the group and its members.

Match the level of self-disclosure to the group's purpose and setting. In most cases, it is best to use low-risk disclosures, such as name, workplace, and hobbies. Deeper levels of sharing can be used later, after trust has developed, if appropriate for the group's purpose and setting. For example, volunteers in training for a hospice program will expect to share feelings about working with dying patients because this is essential for achieving the goals of the program, but employees at a staff development workshop should not be asked to share feelings about working with a boss or coworker.

Be sensitive to cultural diversity. Make sure activities, examples, and language are culturally sensitive to diverse members of the group. Make space for people to be different and be accepted. Watch for individuals who may withdraw from group participation because of cultural conflicts or mistrust of the dominant racial/ethnic group. If possible, invite individuals to share differences openly, and create new ways of handling dilemmas raised in the group.

26 NAME CLAPS

Participants clap out the beats of syllables in their own name and learn the names of partners with similar rhythms.

Goals

To learn names of other participants.

To share personal history related to names.

Time

5–10 minutes

Process

1. After welcoming participants to the group, invite everyone to join in a short get-acquainted game using name claps as a means of introduction. Demonstrate methods of clapping the beats of each syllable of your own first name and then ask all participants to create their own name clap and find others with similar rhythms.

   ■ Stand up and clap out a beat representing the syllables of your first name. Sue would clap once, David would clap twice, Caroline would clap three times, and Maralisa would clap four times.

   ■ Continue clapping your beat over and over as you mill around the room and find other people clapping the same name rhythm.

   ■ Stay with the people who have the same beat as you and keep moving around the room in a cluster, searching for other people whose beat matches yours. Keep moving as a unit until everyone with similar beats has found each other and then stay together in a circle.

2. When four distinct clapping groups have formed, provide new instructions for learning names.

   ■ Starting with the tallest member of the group, introduce yourself by clapping the syllables of your first name while repeating it out loud.

- The person immediately to the left of the first person repeats the clap and the first name of the person, followed by the second person and so on around the circle until everyone has clapped the beat and repeated the first person's name.

- The second person then claps their own beat and states their own first name, and again there is a round robin of claps and repetitions.

Repeat this process until each person has had a chance to do their own name clap and have it repeated around the circle.

3. After all name claps have been completed, ask participants to get acquainted further by clapping the syllables of their last name, finding a partner within the group, and sharing name stories on a one-to-one basis.

- Remain standing in your small group circle and start clapping the syllables of your last name.

- Find someone within your group who has the last name rhythm as you, and pair up with this person. Step apart from the group and find a place to sit down together.

   ☞ *If there are odd numbers in any given group, tell people to join another pair and make a threesome.*

- Exchange first and last names and then tell each other something about your last name, such as its meaning or history, your feelings about it, or your cultural or ethnic heritage.

- Each person has two minutes to share.

4. Signal when time is up and invite people to return to their seats. Comment briefly on the positive effects of learning each other's names and challenge participants to see how many names they can learn and remember during the remainder of the session.

Variations

1. Use original name clap groups to create break-out discussion (or task) groups later on in the session: one-clap, two-clap, three-clap, and four-clap groups.

2. Keeping everyone in a large group, ask people to introduce themselves using a counting method, one-two-three-four, by clapping once and having someone with a one-clap name stand up and clap out their name, followed by a two-clap name and so on, over and over, until everyone has stood, clapped and said their name. For fun, speed up the process, going faster and faster until people collapse in laughter.

LEARNING NAMES À LA CARTE

27 NAMESAKE

1. Ask participants to think of a famous person whom they admire, one with the same first name as their own.

2. Go around the circle, allowing people 1 minute each to introduce themselves, tell about their famous namesake, state why they admire this person, and mention one thing (besides a name) they have in common with this person.

28 RHYMING NAMES

1. Everyone sits in a circle. The starter says her name, rhyming it with a familiar object or adjective, for example, Alan gallon, Sue shoe, Bill gill, Esther pester, George forge, etc.

2. The first person's name rhyme is repeated around the circle.

3. The next person says his name and rhymes it. This new rhyme is repeated around the circle, and the process continues until everyone has been introduced with a rhyme.

29 NAME ECHO

1. Everyone stands in a circle facing the center.

2. The first person says her name and makes a sound or movement that suits her at the moment, for example, Mary cheers "ta-daaaah!" Frank snores, or Fred shrugs his shoulders.

3. The second person repeats the name and mimics the sound or movement made by the first person. This continues around the group like an echo, with each person repeating the name and sound or movement exactly.

4. The second person then introduces herself with her name and a new sound or movement, and the process continues until everyone has been introduced.

30 NAME WAVE

1. This activity is very similar to Name Echo, but the first person says the name of the person next to him and adds a wave

©2003 Whole Person Associates 210 W Michigan Duluth MN 55802 (800) 247-6789

gesture with his arms, which everyone repeats in sequence until it comes back around to the person introduced.

2. The person just introduced now introduces the person next to him and creates a new wave, which goes around the group.

3. Each person takes a turn until there are waves of recognition for everyone in the group.

31 NICKNAMES

1. Pair up with another person and discuss your nicknames: tell where and when you got them and if they lasted. Share your feelings about them.

2. Allow 2 minutes per person.

32 ACRONYMS

Props: three-by-five-inch index cards

1. On an index card, print your first name across the top in clear, legible letters about 1 inch high.

2. For each letter of your name, write in vertical columns a positive adjective to describe yourself, starting with that letter, for example, DAN: diligent, amiable, nice.

3. Create a bolo-tie name-tag by punching holes in the upper corners of the card, running a piece of yarn through each hole, and tying it in a necklace length around your neck.

4. Stand up and mill around the group, introducing yourself and sharing personal acronyms with at least three people.

GETTING ISSUES ON THE TABLE

Whether in work teams, therapy groups, or workshops, people often need structure to overcome initial interpersonal awkwardness and get focused on an issue or direction.

GROUP DYNAMICS PRINCIPLES

Having an agenda helps people make personal applications. When people are focused on a specific agenda, goal, situation, or issue, they personalize content and are more likely to make applications to their own life—making learning relevant, meaningful, and worthwhile.

Everyone gets "air time." It's important that each person has the opportunity to say out loud or affirm something they want to work on. Talking about personal and group agendas is risk-taking that sets the stage for active, responsible participation.

Agendas provide context for evaluation. Individuals can evaluate personal progress: "Did I reach my goals?" while groups can evaluate their effectiveness: "Did we achieve our purpose, accomplish our task?" Without a clear agenda, people won't know if they reached their goals or accomplished anything.

Agendas enable participants to find common ground. Agendas serve as levelers—despite differences in status, background, age, and education, participants subscribe to a common goal or purpose. Everyone gets on board and agrees to head in the same direction.

Setting agendas creates opportunities to address inappropriate expectations. Every group member has personal agendas or motivations for coming to the group. Some are appropriate; some are not. Inappropriate, hidden agendas disrupt the group process, so it's best to get them out in the open and clarify what the group will and will not address.

Leadership styles affect the agenda-setting process. Autocratic leaders determine the group's agenda in advance; democratic leaders involve the group in agenda-setting or negotiate some goals. Both styles have advantages and disadvantages: autocratic groups are the most efficient, but group morale may be low, while democratic groups are likely to be cohesive and satisfying to group members, yet not necessarily more productive. Regardless of leadership style, all groups need an agenda.

TIPS FOR PLANNING AND IMPLEMENTATION

Model brevity, clarity, and specificity. Start by stating your own agenda (personal or professional) for the group. Then check participant responses to this agenda—does your agenda for the group match the expectations of participants? Be sure to get your ground rules settled as part of this process (listening, respect for divergent viewpoints, no unsolicited feedback, everyone participates, etc.).

In large groups, restate or summarize each contribution. This affirms individuals and establishes good, clear communication.

Record agenda items on a whiteboard or newsprint. When the list of agenda items is complete, use the list to clarify the agenda by starring key items and crossing out those that are inappropriate (offer ideas about where to get these needs met). Having a visual summary makes goals clear and concrete.

If necessary, use agenda-consensus methods. One way of building consensus is to have participants anonymously write goals on three-by-five inch index cards (one per card) and give them to the leader, who reads them aloud and records them on a whiteboard. The leader then assigns a number to each item and asks group members to silently pick their favorite goal and vote for it by raising their hand when that number is called. Items with the greatest number of votes are adopted unless there is strong opposition to them, in which case they are negotiated or modified to satisfy participants.

Ask participants to write a learning contract. When people pledge in writing to work on specific goals, they are more likely to stick to them.

Put up a quote to set the tone for agenda setting. Posting a provocative statement, such as "Groups always underestimate their own human resources," can be a powerful catalyst, inspiring groups to set ambitious, yet attainable goals.

CAUTIONS

Discussion may reveal conflicts. In rare cases, discussion of agendas will uncover a wide, irreconcilable difference between an individual's agenda and the group's agenda, causing someone to withdraw from the group. While this can be embarrassing and awkward or make you feel like you failed, it can be seen as testimony to the effectiveness of the agenda-setting process. If the group is truly a poor fit for an individual, it is better to separate gracefully than to proceed with a conflict you know will only result in disappointment, frustration, and anger.

It is not ethical to keep your agenda hidden from the group. Participants have the right to know what activities you have planned for the group and their purpose so they can make informed decisions about participation. It's fine to keep it fairly general so you don't steal your own thunder—just inform group members about the activity and what will be expected of them.

Stay focused on agreed-upon agendas. Don't get sidetracked by issues that you have strong feelings about or allow yourself to be swayed by emotions of other group members. Stay focused, watch the time, and keep things moving.

SPECIAL CONSIDERATIONS FOR ONGOING GROUPS

Ongoing groups share a history that is different from time-limited groups. While all groups need a way to focus, ongoing groups need a bridge for linking past to present—a refresher—and a structure for reconnecting. This provides continuity for group members, and an opportunity to renew commitment.

It's important to provide a process for including new members or someone who was absent at the last meeting. When everyone has to respond to the same question or process, each person is on the same footing or level. This is especially important with ongoing groups because information is power, and only by sharing information can there be equal power between old and new members.

Checking in at the beginning of each group session gives participants the opportunity to brag about what's gone well. It's rewarding to see personal progress toward goals and to receive affirmation and support for individual effort. By giving each person time to talk about gains made since the last meeting, groups reinforce growth in their members.

Ongoing groups need periodic shake-ups of the status quo. All groups are at risk for getting stuck, falling into a rut, losing sight of purpose or goals, failing to resolve conflicts, or getting confused about roles and responsibilities.

To shake things up and reorganize in a healthy way, make time on the agenda to talk about how things are going. Ask provocative questions: "What would you like to do as a member of this group that you've never had the opportunity to do before?" or "Do you feel your needs, skills, and interests are utilized in this group?" These questions will provide needed structure and stimulus for group housecleaning, sweeping away resentments and frustrations and opening the door for a fresh start.

33 ADMISSION TICKET

When participants arrive, they are given an admission ticket, and asked to register by writing on their ticket why they should be coming to this course.

Goals

To clarify personal goals and motivations.

To facilitate the development of a group agenda.

Materials Needed

Worksheet: *Admission Ticket* (page 45) newsprint or white-board.

Time

10–15 minutes

Process

1. As participants arrive, give them a worksheet and ask them to indicate on the ticket why they are coming to the course.

   ■ On your admission ticket, write all the reasons why you should be coming to this course.

   ■ Write one or two things you hope to learn or gain from coming to this group.

2. Form groups of four and ask participants to formally seek admission to the group by showing their ticket and talking about their motivations for coming to this course.

   ■ Starting with the person wearing the most colorful socks, go around the group and seek admission by showing your admission ticket and completing the following sentence: "I should be admitted to this course because . . ."

   ■ Tell what you hope to learn or gain from the course also.

3. When everyone has displayed a ticket in the small groups, give the groups the task of developing a common group goal or agenda item.

   ■ Find a goal you have in common for this course, something

you are all interested in learning today.

■ You have three minutes to discuss and agree on a common goal or agenda item.

■ The person with the darkest socks is group reporter and will share your common goal with the large group.

4. After three minutes, stop the discussions and invite group reporters to share the common goals of their group with the large group. Write group goals on a whiteboard or newsprint, putting a star beside goals that are mentioned by more than one group.

5. Summarize common goals and interests of the group and then clarify which goals will be addressed by the group and which will not. If necessary, lead a discussion on how to modify goals and agree on priorities for the day.

AGENDA SETTERS À LA CARTE

34 TRANSITIONS

1. Ask participants to join one of three groups, depending on what stage of life transition they are experiencing: an ending stage, an in-between stage, or a new beginning stage.

2. Invite everyone to take one minute to introduce themselves and tell what factors made them place themselves in this transition stage. Then have the group brainstorm a list of ways that being in this stage of life or transition affects interests, goals, and attitudes about participating in this group. The person with the newest car should act as reporter, writing down all ideas and reporting back to the large group.

3. Invite group reporters to share the effects of life-stage transitions on their group's interests, attitudes, and issues. Summarize common themes and goals.

35 I CALLED THE SHERIFF

Worksheet: *I Called the Sheriff* (page 46)

1. Give everyone a worksheet and ask people to reflect individually on where they need to police themselves, where they need rescue, and how they convict themselves. Instruct participants to write responses on their worksheet.

2. Have participants join a small group and share their "policing" issues.

3. Reconvene the group and ask for volunteers to share examples of responses to each question. Summarize common issues and weave them into a discussion about the group's agenda.

36 DOZEN GIFTS

Worksheet: *Dozen Gifts* (page 47)

1. Distribute worksheets and invite participants to reflect on gifts they'd like to receive and gifts they'd like to give. Ask them to write a dozen gift ideas on their worksheet, one in each gift box.

2. Tell participants to form triads and take turns sharing their dozen gifts.

3. Poll the group for examples of gifts participants want to give and receive, encouraging everyone to consider the potential of giving and receiving some of these gifts today, during the rest of the workshop. Gifts of laughter, good humor, and appreciation are welcome.

Variation: Make this a closing exercise, and have participants give and receive gifts during a farewell ceremony.

37 TAKE A CLOSE LOOK

Worksheet: *Take a Close Look* (page 48)

1. Give everyone a worksheet. Invite participants to reflect on what needs attention in their life and write personal reflections on their magnifying glass.

2. Create small groups and have everyone introduce themselves by holding up their magnifying glass and telling what needs their close attention.

3. Solicit examples of the things participants think need attention in their life and relate these issues to the group's agenda.

38 POISON

Worksheet: *Poison* (page 49)

1. Hand out worksheets and invite participants to think about what some of their poisons are—for example, people, situations, attitudes, activities, or feelings. These can be physical poisons, relationship poisons, work poisons, etc.—anything that is deadly or destructive for them. They should write their poisons in the bottle on their worksheet.

2. Tell participants to find a partner and share their poisons.

3. Reconvene the group and make a list of poisons shared by group members. Then talk about how the group's activities or learning agenda may provide antidotes for some of these poisons.

39 APRIL SHOWERS

Worksheet: *April Showers* (page 50)

1. Give each person a worksheet and ask them to reflect on what's showering down on them and how they protect

themselves from the deluge. In the sky, they should write all the things showering down on them; under the umbrella, they should write ways they protect themselves.

2. Create small groups and instruct participants to take turns telling about their April showers and ways they protect themselves from the deluge. Two minutes each.

3. Reconvene the large group and invite volunteers to share examples of ways they protect themselves from getting soaked by April showers.

40 WHISK BROOM

Worksheet: *Whisk Broom* (page 51)

1. Invite participants to reflect on areas of their life they need to sweep clean or areas of their life needing housecleaning, along with things they are sweeping under the rug and not paying attention to. Hand out worksheets and direct participants to write reflections on their worksheet.

2. Form four-member groups and ask participants to take two minutes each to share what they noted about their life-cleaning issues and challenges.

3. Reconvene the large group and lead a discussion about ways the group might help with cleaning/sweeping agendas or in getting issues out from under the rug.

41 UNFINISHED BUSINESS

1. As an opener for ongoing groups, form small groups to discuss unfinished business from the last session.

2. Reconvene the group and invite people to share their progress in settling unfinished business. Guide the larger group in further discussion of unfinished business if needed for resolution. Then move on to the next item on the agenda.

42 BELL RINGERS

Worksheet: *Bell Ringers* (page 52)

1. After a brief chalktalk about how easy it is to get distracted, ask participants to stop and listen to their internal bell, which

may be ringing for attention. Give some examples. (Bell ringers may be physical symptoms, like a pain in the neck or mental signals, such as a nagging worry, the alarm of bad dreams, or the shock of unexpected feedback.) Give everyone a worksheet, asking them to record inside the bell the messages their internal warning system is sending them. Below the bell, they should write how they need to respond to the bell-ringing message, along with any support they may require to make this response.

2. Have participants form small groups and tell about their personal bell ringers and their current needs.

4. As volunteers share examples of personal needs, list them on newsprint, hanging the list for reference during the day. At some later time, share information about community resources that may be helpful.

43 BUGLE CALL

Worksheet: *Bugle Call* (page 53)

1. Distribute worksheets and ask participants to think about what they need to wake up to:

- What challenges are calling them

- In what ways do they need to prepare for battle, and

- What are they putting to rest or playing "Taps" for.

Tell people to write their reflections on their worksheet.

2. Assign participants to small groups and instruct them to go around the group and answer the bugle call by sharing as much as they choose about their personal wake-up calls, challenges, battles, defeats, surrenders, or letting-go experiences.

3. Call the group back together and talk about common challenges and battles faced by group members and how the course agenda relates to these experiences.

44 RESISTANCE

Worksheet: *Resistance Questionnaire* (page 54)

1. Give everyone a worksheet and invite people to think about their usual reactions to potential change (in their workplace,

at home, in their personal routines, etc.). Ask them to rank from 1 to 10 their typical reasons for resisting change, with 1 being their strongest or most common reason for resisting change and 10 being their weakest or least common reason.

2. Tell participants to share their resistance rankings with a partner, and then conduct a survey to find out the most common methods of resistance in your group. Engage participants in lighthearted problem-solving on ways to eliminate these learning blocks.

45 I HOPE TO ACCOMPLISH

1. Assign everyone to a small group. Ask members to discuss what they hope to accomplish in the session and report back to the large group.

2. Listen to what each group hopes to accomplish and then lead a discussion about goals, sorting out realistic and unrealistic ones.

46 SIGNS OF MY TIMES

Worksheet: *Signs of My Times* (page 55)

1. Give participants worksheets and ask them to make signs representing how they limit themselves (for example, "Change Resisted Here" or "If at First You Don't Succeed, Give Up").

2. Create a human billboard highway by having half the group stand along a wall and hold up their signs, while other group members walk along the highway and read the signs. Reverse roles so the remaining participants can show their signs.

3. Tell participants to grab a partner and share values represented by their signs.

Variation: Change the theme of the billboards to match your goals (for example, changes I'm trying to make or my current attitude at work).

47 REMEMBER ME

1. Create small groups. Ask participants to take turns telling what they would most like to be remembered for after they die. In a second round, ask them to tell what they want to be

©2003 Whole Person Associates 210 W Michigan Duluth MN 55802 (800) 247-6789

remembered for today, as a group member.

2. Encourage participants to let their desire for remembrance by other group members—which may be an important personal goal—guide them in how they choose to participate.

48 MEGAPHONE

Props: Small megaphone or paper cup with the bottom removed for each small group

1. Have participants gather in small groups and seat themselves in circles. Ask them to think about what they would like to speak up about—to shout more loudly (a complaint, an affirmation, or an exhortation).

2. Invite people to speak up by taking turns declaring their message clearly to the rest of the group, using the megaphone. Demonstrate with your own message and then pass a megaphone to one member in each group.

3. Repeat the process, this time focusing on a message people need to hear more strongly. Invite people, in return, to reverse the megaphone, hold it up to their ear, and tell what they need to hear more loudly. If appropriate, invite the rest of the group to join in a unison repetition of each person's message.

49 NEST EGG

Worksheet: *Nest Egg* (page 56)

1. Give everyone worksheets and ask them to write on the eggs things that need nurturing in their lives or resources waiting to hatch. When finished, they should share their nest eggs with a partner.

2. Ask the large group to brainstorm a list of what conditions, environment, actions, and attitudes would help their eggs or resources hatch or come to life. Incorporate their ideas into the group ground rules and the workshop agenda.

50 RUBBER GLOVES

Props: Several rubber gloves, enough so there is a glove for each small group

1. Ask participants to form small groups and distribute a glove to each group. As the glove is passed from one person to another, members should talk for two minutes each about the things from which they need to protect themselves, both inside and outside the group.

2. Reconvene the group and ask participants to share examples of protection needs inside the group. Use this as a springboard for a discussion about ground rules.

51 WINNING HAND

Worksheet: *Winning Hand* (page 57)

1. Begin by talking about how every person is dealt a different hand in life—family of origin, financial resources, health issues, stressors, etc.

2. Give each participant a worksheet and a playing card. Ask people to identify and note some of the cards they have been dealt in life.

3. Note that whatever hand of cards we've been dealt, we decide how to play it. Ask people to jot some notes about how they intend to play their hand (work hard, keep a sense of humor, be extra careful about diet, avoid stressful situations, etc.).

4. Create several small "card clubs," grouping people by their playing card (all spades or all face cards or all 8s, for example).

5. Reconvene the large group and remind participants that no matter the hand they've been dealt, they always have a choice about how they're going to play.

52 HANG-UPS

Worksheet: *Hang-Ups* (page 58)

1. Give everyone a worksheet and invite people to identify personal hang-ups that need work.

2. Tell participants to find a partner and take turns sharing hang-ups, without judging each other or giving advice. Participants should just listen to each other and affirm their partner for taking risks and sharing hang-ups.

©2003 Whole Person Associates 210 W Michigan Duluth MN 55802 (800) 247-6789

53 ERASER

Worksheet: *Eraser* (page 59)

1. Ask participants to reflect on actions taken at home or work that they would like to forget or wish they could undo. Distribute worksheets and ask people to record some of these mistakes or regretted actions.

2. Form triads and tell participants to take turns sharing examples of mistakes or actions they wish they could delete from memory. People should refrain from advice-giving and simply listen to one another.

3. Lead a large-group discussion about how participants can erase—or let go of—past mistakes and focus on positive actions they can take in the present.

54 I'M PUZZLED

Worksheet: *I'm Puzzled* (page 60)

1. After a full-length presentation, pause for questions. Distribute worksheets and instruct group members to write an impromptu list of questions they have so far.

2. Form groups of eight. Tell participants to take turns reading their questions, allowing other group members to respond to each question in one minute or less. Each person should have a chance to ask at least one question and hear answers or responses from the group.

Admit One

Reasons why I should come to this course:

_____

_____

_____

_____

_____

_____

_____

Things I hope to learn or gain from this group experience:

_____

_____

_____

_____

_____

I Called the Sheriff

Where do I need to police myself?

_____

_____

_____

_____

Where do I need rescue?

_____

_____

_____

_____

How do I convict myself?

_____

_____

_____

_____

Dozen Gifts

What gifts would you like to receive or to give?
Write one gift in each gift box.

Take a Close Look

Look at your life and yourself with a magnifying glass.
What needs attention?

Poison

What are some of your poisons?

People	Situations	Attitudes	Activities
Feelings	Physical	Work	Relationships

List them on the bottle.

April Showers

Above the umbrella, write the things that are showering down on you.

Below the umbrella, write how you protect yourself from the deluge.

Whisk Broom

Where do I need to sweep clean?
What areas of my life need housecleaning?
What am I sweeping under the rug?

Bell Ringers

On the bell, write what is trying to get your attention?

What message does the bell ringer have for you?

_____

How do you need to respond?

_____

What support do you require?

_____

Bugle Call

What do you need to wake up to?

_____

_____

What challenges are calling you?

_____

_____

Where do you need to prepare for battle?

_____

_____

For what things in your life are you blowing "Taps"?

_____

_____

Resistance

Rank these common reasons for resisting change according to your typical reaction. #1 should be your most common reason, #10 the least common.

_____ See no reason to change

_____ Uncertain of purpose of change

_____ Too much work or trouble

_____ Worry about how other people will react

_____ Not sure of reasons for change

_____ Past experience with change

_____ Expect the change will fail

_____ Fear the change will succeed

_____ Not sure what changes are really needed

_____ Too many unknown consequences

Signs of My Times

Nest Egg

In each egg, list something that needs nurturing in your life or a resource waiting to hatch.

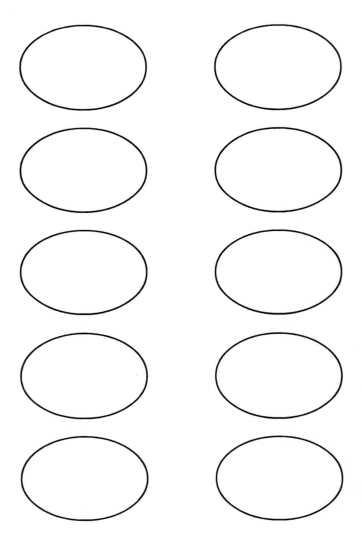

Winning Hand

On each card in the hand, write the cards that you
have been dealt. Consider, for example, stressors, resources,
family of origin issues, and health problems.

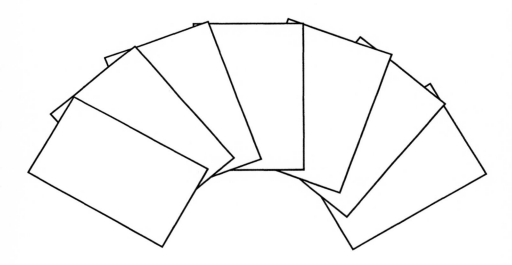

How will you play your cards?

_____

_____

_____

Hang-Ups

What personal hang-ups need work?

Eraser

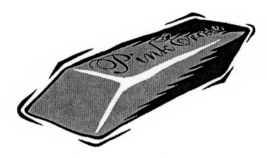

What mistakes or regretted actions would you like to erase?

_____

_____

_____

_____

_____

_____

_____

_____

_____

I'm Puzzled

I'm puzzled about . . .

_____

_____

_____

_____

_____

_____

_____

_____

_____

_____

_____

_____

_____

_____

MAIN COURSE

Group Building Processes

Conversation Starters

Tools for Self-Awareness

Discussions & Brainstorming

Analogies & Metaphors

Creative Activities

GROUP BUILDING PROCESSES

All icebreakers are intended to help build group connections and a sense of shared purpose and common experience among participants. Beyond making introductions and learning names, icebreakers can be beneficial to continued group-building during a session, workshop, course, or ongoing group. Be intentional about group building, whatever the setting. Make group goals, membership, and activities attractive to everyone so people will be eager to participate from beginning to end and will be rewarded for participation by satisfying group experiences.

GROUP DYNAMICS PRINCIPLES

Participants must be attracted to each other. Social attraction (not romantic or physical) is an important variable in group development. Not everyone will like everyone else, but participants will almost always enjoy a few other group members. Because we tend to like people who like us, these attractions become mutually reinforcing, creating sympathetic bonds and feelings of trust that can and do multiply.

Participants must be attracted to group goals. Group goals are the very reason for the group's existence, so it's important that they are based on values important to participants. Learn what individual group members consider worth pursuing and keep this purpose clear in the minds of participants.

Participants must be attracted to group activities. When membership in a group is voluntary, people come to it because they perceive the group's activities as desirable, either as ends in themselves—for example, enjoying discussions in a support group—or as a means to an end—for example, joining a class to strengthen parenting skills. To prevent members from mentally or physically withdrawing from the group, keep activities interesting and relevant.

Progressive intimacy and self-disclosure. When pairs discuss an issue, then join in quartets and introduce each other and discuss another aspect of the topic, then join in groups of eight for another round of sharing, the ripple effects of self-disclosure and active listening touch more people, and the group becomes more cohesive.

Building group consensus. Exercises like values ranking or finding common agenda items, build group consensus, which in turn promotes cohesion and commitment. Because some modification of individual behavior is necessary in order to conform to the goals or actions of the group, building group consensus is an effective way to move things in this direction.

Working together, solving problems. Given a task such as writing a song, solving a puzzle, or brainstorming ten strategies for dealing with teenagers, groups use creativity to accomplish the assignment and in doing so work effectively as a team, helping individuals define their roles and share their personal skills. Success brings satisfaction and pride in the group's accomplishment and makes teamwork rewarding.

Shared trauma or difficulty. Outdoor challenge courses, timed stressful situations, confessions of addictions or abuse, and other shared difficulties can bring people together and create a sense of universal experience that unites individuals as a group.

Group-building is an ongoing activity. Groups can't rest on their past accomplishments; they must strive for greater teamwork, be willing to engage in introspection and feedback, (giving and receiving openness, trust, spontaneity, mutuality, sharing, risk-taking, experimentation, and care for one another), and keep growing.

TIPS FOR PLANNING AND IMPLEMENTATION

Be sure you really want to build group identity. It has potential disadvantages—cliques, dependency, exclusiveness, us versus them, power dynamics, "group think," and disruptive norms—as well as benefits—connections, cooperation, identification, synergy, support, purpose, and belonging.

If you allow time for formation and connection, you need to allow similar time for disconnecting or disbanding. People need rituals for leaving, for saying good-bye, for reflecting on the outside world, and for thinking about what they will take home from the group.

In longer workshops, you may want to rotate groups. No one should get stuck for the whole time in a group that doesn't jell. Upsetting the apple cart brings surprises that many people find invigorating—and not just those who were dissatisfied with their old group! Change brings fresh possibilities for everyone.

©1998 Whole Person Associates 210 W Michigan Duluth MN 55802 (800) 247-6789

Physical environment affects group communication. Everyone has horror stories about times that physical surroundings were not suited for good communication, when the effects of paper-thin walls, crowded space, poor lighting, inadequate ventilation, noise pollution, and other factors weakened the energy of the group. Plan ahead and create an environment that fits your group's needs.

Begin by discussing the group's purpose and expectations. Inviting participants to give input into group activities, goals, and ground rules makes the group a joint effort from the very beginning. Shared responsibility is a hallmark of successful groups.

Attend to the feelings of group members. Listen to feelings expressed by group members, verbally and nonverbally, and respond appropriately. For example, "I can see people are getting tired, so let's take a break."

CAUTIONS

Don't sacrifice the agenda to the process. If small groups aren't working, try pairs or trios or alternate with a few large group activities or use journals for individual reflection.

If group dynamics are building in unhealthy ways, break up the patterns. Physically move people around; switch to different size groups; change the pace with a different kind of activity; take a stretch break; or restate the ground rules.

Be sensitive to minority group members' issues about trust. Past experiences with oppression and racism may make minority group members reluctant to trust majority group members, or vice versa. If possible, talk about these issues openly and if conflicts emerge, maintain a problem-solving focus.

©1998 Whole Person Associates 210 W Michigan Duluth MN 55802   (800) 247-6789

55 EITHER/OR

Participants choose between opposite values by symbolically placing themselves on different sides of the room, depending on what values they ascribe to, and then sharing conspicuous values with other participants.

Goals

To raise awareness of value issues in making choices.

To expose participants to choices and thoughts of other participants and promote interaction about these choices.

Time

10–15 minutes

Process

This should be a fast-paced mixer; don't let things get bogged down during discussions. Use a horn or harmonica to signal times to switch partners.

1. In advance, select a topic and prepare a list of either/or opposites that represent choices about the topic. For example, if the topic is health, the opposites might be: too healthy or too sick, too fat or too thin, alfalfa sprouts or a Big Mac, ice cream or yogurt, TV or bicycle, too aggressive or too passive, too social or too solitary.

2. Ask everyone to stand in the middle of the room. Read aloud the first either/or question. Repeat it, pointing to a side of the room for each alternative and instructing participants to go to the side representing their value.

   ▪ Which of these two opposites do you most identify with: too healthy or too sick?

   ▪ Go to the wall representing your choice.

   ▪ Look around and notice the participants who share your choice on this value and then return to the middle of the room.

3. Read aloud another either/or choice, and repeat the process in step two, moving quickly through about ten choices.

4. Instruct participants to pair up and share their experiences.

   ▪ Find someone who made some of the same choices as you and share reasons for your choices.

   ▪ Each person has two minutes to share.

5. Interrupt the discussions and invite people to move to a new partner.

   ▪ Now find someone who made a choice different from you.

   ▪ Take one minute each and share reasons for your choices.

6. Stop the discussions again and encourage participants to try and guess someone else's choice.

   ▪ Pair up with another person whose choices you do not know and try to guess their answer to one of the questions.

   ▪ Each person takes a turn guessing and then shares reasons for choices.

7. Ask pairs to form groups of six and continue sharing.

   ▪ Join two other pairs to make a group of six and sit down together.

   ▪ Discuss similarities and differences in your values choices and share reasons for similarities and differences.

8. After about five minutes, end the discussion and invite each group to share what they discovered about their values and about their similarities to and differences from other participants.

Variation

Instead of listing choices related to the topic, try a list of either/ or values choices that affect group participation: shy or outgoing, passive or active, serious or playful, leader or follower, open or closed, enthusiastic or apathetic. In small groups, discuss how these values affect group participation.

GROUP BUILDERS À LA CARTE

56 REMINISCENCE

Worksheet: *Photo Album* (page 73)

1. Give each person a worksheet. Ask group members to think back to their childhood and recall:

   ▪ their happiest memory

   ▪ their least happy or most embarrassing memory

   ▪ something which made them proud

   ▪ something they really liked

   ▪ something they really disliked

   They should write these memories in the corresponding snapshot of their photo album. Make up a sixth memory question if you want or ask participants to add another reminiscence to their album.

2. Direct participants to form pairs or small groups, and share memories.

Variation: For a powerful closing exercise (most suitable for long workshops or ongoing groups), substitute group memories for childhood memories.

57 BUILDING BLOCKS

Props: colorful blocks, marbles, poker chips, slips of paper, or balloons

1. Put different colored blocks in a box and ask each person to pick a cube, join a group with other participants who have the same color block, and learn each other's names.

2. Ask participants to exchange their blocks for a different color and repeat the process, or have each group introduce itself to the others.

58 TREASURE HUNT

For groups of 30 or more.

Worksheet: *Treasure Hunt* (page 74)

©1998 Whole Person Associates 210 W Michigan Duluth MN 55802   (800) 247-6789

1. Give each person a worksheet and invite people to get acquainted and discover the resources (treasures) of the group by finding people who match the descriptions on the list. Give guidelines for the hunt:
   ▪ Put each human treasure's name in the space provided
   ▪ Only two treasures per customer (no hogging)
   ▪ Start with someone not presently sitting next to you
2. After six to eight minutes (depending on the energy level of the group), ask people to join with two other nearby folks and discuss whatever topic is next on the agenda (the best and worst ways to manage stress, strategies for handling toddlers, ideas for improving morale in your workplace, etc.).
3. Bring the whole group back together for reports from the trios.

59 STRESS IS . . .

1. Instruct participants to form triads and make up funny definitions for stress or specific classifications of stress, such as physical stressors, conflict situations, family strains, or life events.
2. Ask each group to read its definition aloud to the entire group.

60 SITUATIONS AND SUGGESTIONS

1. Ask the entire group to help brainstorm a list of challenging life or work situations or dilemmas. Record ideas on newsprint as they are generated.
2 Based on your goals for the session and the issues raised by the group, choose several situations and make a newsprint poster for each challenge.
2. Form groups with three members and invite the groups to walk around the room, stopping at each newsprint poster to discuss strategies for handling that situation. The should write three possible strategies for responding on any empty poster and two suggestions on the others.
3. Reconvene the group and discuss creative response strategies to the variety of life challenges we face.

61 MISSION STATEMENT

Worksheet: *Mission Statement* (page 75)

1. Give everyone a worksheet. Tell them to complete the sentence stubs and then write a statement that incorporates the meaning of all four sentences.

2. Form small groups. Instruct participants to read their mission statements aloud to each other and then merge ideas to create another mission statement—one that is inspirational for everyone in the group.

3. Invite each group to read its mission statement and then post them on a wall for inspiration.

62 LISTENING

Make a list of controversial, provocative stimulus statements related to your topic (for example, "Every organization should self-destruct every five years." "Absence makes the heart grow fonder—of being absent." "The best man for the job is a woman."). Write each key phrase on a three-by-five-inch index card.

1. Form groups of three and announce that each person will have an opportunity to respond to a provocative statement that you will read. Give instructions to groups:

   ■ Decide who will be first.

   ■ Each person will take a turn being the focus of the group's attention for two minutes, during which time they can respond to the statement however they choose (agreeing, criticizing, praising, summarizing), while the other two people focus their attention totally on the person sharing— restraining or curbing their own reactions until it's their time to be the focus person.

   ■ Listeners should experiment with acceptance of the focus person, even if they disagree, and with offering nonverbal signs of listening.

2. Read the first stimulus statement. After two minutes, announce that the person to the left responds next. Read the next statement. Continue until everyone has had a turn.

63 GROUP QUILT

Props: a ten-inch square of white cloth and colored markers for each participant, poster board for each small group

1. As people arrive, give them a cloth square and markers. Tell them to write their first name on the cloth and draw or write something unique that they bring to the group, such as a sense of humor, or seventy years of life experience.

2. Form groups of six people and invite participants to introduce themselves, using their quilt patch. When finished, ask them to glue their patches to poster board, which becomes the group's quilt and is displayed on an easel or hung on a wall.

64 IN THE NEIGHBORHOOD

1. Ask participants to join one of three groups, depending on the type of neighborhood they grew up in: farm/rural, small town, or big city/suburb. Invite them to get acquainted by sharing advantages and disadvantages of growing up in this type of neighborhood.

2. Tell each group to appoint a committee of two (the persons with the shortest and longest last names). Direct them to visit one of the other neighborhoods and interview its members about advantages and disadvantages of growing up in their neighborhood.

3. Reconvene the group and ask the teams to report what they learned.

65 BODY CONVERSATION

1. Divide the large group into groups of four to six people. Invite participants to introduce themselves and explain their moods—using body language only—while the rest of the group tries to guess what they are saying.

66 MOVING QUESTIONS

1. Invite participants to sit in a circle facing the center and get acquainted by taking turns asking another person in the group one moving question—any question that can be answered with a "yes" or "no" response. When someone answers "yes," everyone moves one seat to the right of that person;

when someone answers "no," everyone moves one seat to the left. Slowpokes risk getting sat upon by other participants. Pick someone to start. The person who answers the first question gets to ask the next one.

67 PUT-DOWNS AND AFFIRMATIONS

Props: a balloon and a three-foot piece of string for each person

1. Give everyone a balloon and a string. Tell them to blow up their balloon and then tie it to one of their ankles. Invite everyone to walk around and stomp on other people's balloons until every balloon is popped. Tell participants to pay attention to their feelings when their own balloon is popped and when they pop someone else's balloon.

2. Instruct participants to form groups of three and share feelings about having their balloons popped and about popping other's balloons. Ask them to continue by discussing how they feel when their psychic balloon is popped at home, school, or elsewhere.

3. When everyone has shared, ask people to go around the group again, giving each person a genuine compliment or affirmation. Ask groups to discuss their feelings when receiving affirmations rather than put-downs.

68 DIALOG

Handout: *Dialog Questions* (page 76)

1. Tell participants to pair up with someone who seems different from them in some way. Distribute handouts and instruct each pair to take turns asking and responding to questions on the list. Explain that when asking a question, they must first listen to their partner's answers and then answer the same question themselves. Tell people that what they share with partners will be kept confidential and that it is okay to "pass" on any given question. Allow five to ten minutes for dialogs.

Variation: Adapt the *Dialog Questions* handout to elicit responses on issues appropriate to your group and agenda.

©1998 Whole Person Associates 210 W Michigan Duluth MN 55802 (800) 247-6789

69 INTERIOR DECORATORS

1. Divide furniture into equal shares for the number of small groups you have and place each grouping of furniture in the center of the room. Direct each small group to a pile of furniture and tell members to arrange it in any way that pleases the group.

2. When finished, ask each group to relax in their new furniture arrangement and talk about how it feels to be in this new design. Ask participants to compare feelings about old and new arrangements and talk about how it felt to be a group interior decorator.

Photo Album

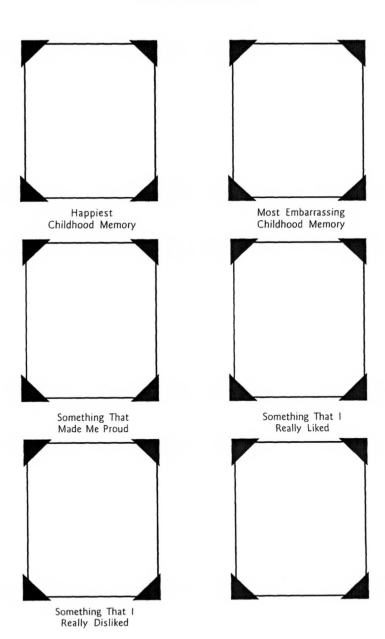

Happiest
Childhood Memory

Most Embarrassing
Childhood Memory

Something That
Made Me Proud

Something That I
Really Liked

Something That I
Really Disliked

Human Treasure Hunt

Find at least two people who:

have freckles   _____   _____

own a truck   _____   _____

voted Democratic in the last election   _____   _____

see themselves as creative   _____   _____

enjoying working with wood   _____   _____

fish   _____   _____

have been to the Grand Canyon   _____   _____

were born in August   _____   _____

consider their job too stressful   _____   _____

LOVE their jobs   _____   _____

moved in the last year   _____   _____

gave up a habit in the last year   _____   _____

pray or meditate daily   _____   _____

think they eat or drink too much   _____   _____

love watching TV   _____   _____

hate watching TV   _____   _____

have the same shoe size as you   _____   _____

came with the same expectations as you   _____   _____

enjoy journaling on a regular basis   _____   _____

are cancer survivors   _____   _____

call themselves desperate parents   _____   _____

describe themselves as a rock of strength _____   _____

©1998 Whole Person Associates 210 W Michigan Duluth MN 55802 (800) 247-6789

Mission Statement

The thing that is unique or special about our group is:

_____

_____

The main purpose or goal of our group is:

_____

_____

The people who will benefit from our group accomplishing our goal are:

_____

_____

My Mission Statement for Our Group

_____

_____

_____

_____

_____

_____

Dialog Questions

What is your most prized material possession?

What are your current personal goals?

What was the greatest turning point of your life?

Do you feel that you have a life purpose? If so, what is it?

What was one of the high points of your life?

What was one of the low points of your life?

Can you accept compliments? Give examples.

If you could live your life over, what would you change?

What personal qualities do you have that you are proud of?

What personal qualities are you ashamed of?

What part of your life do you feel you are most in control of?

What part of your life do you feel least in control of?

What feeling are you most comfortable expressing?

What feeling are you least comfortable expressing?

What do you think you need the most help with?

What kind of help is easiest for you to give to others?

Which of these questions did you like the best?

Which of these questions did you like the least?

©1998 Whole Person Associates 210 W Michigan Duluth MN 55802 (800) 247-6789

CONVERSATION STARTERS

Conversation starters are simple tools for easing people into brief, informal, frank discussions. Use them for getting acquainted, introducing a new topic, and providing a connecting point for group members. Provocative questions help people make immediate, personal application and provide focus, awareness, and context for relating to other group members and to the topic at hand.

GROUP DYNAMICS PRINCIPLES

Conversation starters take the pressure off. Getting to know others makes a lot of people nervous because they aren't sure what to say or how to say it. Having a clear script for conversation allows participants to relax as they simply respond to questions. Knowing that everyone is in the same boat is also reassuring; nobody is alone in the effort to make conversation.

Conversation starters give people connecting points. Brief, personal conversations between two or more people create a link between them, a common reference, a shared understanding, a humorous association, or an interesting discovery. When former partners encounter each other later, they can recall these earlier conversations and enjoy a feeling of camaraderie and support.

Conversation starters assure that everyone will participate. There will always be people who enjoy talking and others who are more comfortable being quiet, but it's a mistake to let the talkers do all the talking, while quiet people fade into the woodwork. Everyone has something to say, and conversation starters are a way to make sure they will have the opportunity to say it.

Sharing can increase self-awareness. In a rapid-fire sequence of conversation starters, questions can surprise people. Off-the-cuff responses are often revealing and bring increased self-awareness, which makes people more responsible group members and enhances the quality of group experience.

Conversation starters provide both one-to-one and group connections. As a mixer, conversation starters give people private time with a series of partners, as well as a sense of connection to the entire group. These experiences build commitment and reinforce personal investment in the group.

Sharing can help others. Allowing others to know us as we see ourselves can open the door to greater understanding and depth in relationships. Others can learn from our experiences and be helped by something we've said or done.

TIPS FOR PLANNING AND IMPLEMENTATION

Decide on the level of self-disclosure appropriate for your group. If you are uncertain about which questions to include and which to leave out, try brainstorming a list of possible disclosures for your group. Review the list and assign a ranking to each disclosure: 1 for low risk, 2 for medium, 3 for high risk. High-risk questions ask people to reveal intimate, personal material that is most likely connected to strong (positive and negative) emotions. While sharing on this level is a powerful way to build intimacy, it is not appropriate for most educational, work, or task groups. Stick with the lower-risk items.

Provide a gradual warm-up to the topic. Ask a series of questions ranging from neutral to emotion-laden, from general to personal, from low to high level self-disclosure, working within clear limits regarding appropriate levels of disclosure for the group.

Use conversation starters as mixers. Pair people up and switch partners for each successive conversation starter. Besides helping participants to know more people, this method keeps things lively and interesting. Doing a mixer early in the session — the earlier the better — will enrich all the group activities that follow.

Remind people to listen without judgment. This is the bread and butter of all good conversation. A few tips or brief reminders on how to give full attention while suspending judgment may be helpful. Make group goals and expectations explicit: diversity enriches the group, and everyone is accepted.

Keep time and provide structure. To keep the sharing moving between partners, around the group, or during partner switches, you need to provide structure by saying who starts first (inner/outer circle, taller persons, etc.). Keep time and interrupt with a whistle, harmonica, or other cue so participants know when to stop or move on to a new partner.

Overcome the leadership vacuum in small groups. Provide an immediate focus or task to resolve the issue of leadership and save time. Designating who will go first (oldest, longest last name, earliest birthday in year, etc.) in a round-robin discussion can prevent debate or attempts to pass the buck. Telling group members to brainstorm a list of ideas on a given topic in four minutes provides the kind of focus the group needs to move ahead. Clear structure, clear instructions—groups need both.

CAUTIONS

Know where you are going. Don't ask frivolous questions as an icebreaker; make sure they will lead people toward your or their goals.

Don't overuse. Too many conversation starters may seem like game-playing instead of real conversation. Structured conversation goes where the leader wants, not where the participants wander. This is an appetizer, not the main course, so keep it short and sweet and be ready to move to a deeper level in your progression.

Make sure people know it's okay to "pass" on sharing. No matter how well you plan what you think are appropriate, nonthreatening conversation starters, some people may not want to respond to certain questions, which they feel are too personal or revealing. Make sure you tell people that it's okay to pass on these questions or to be selective in what they choose to share. People who choose to not share should never be pressured, badgered, or belittled for their decision to be private.

Be sensitive to issues of confidentiality and privacy. Make it clear that personal information about other people stays with the group. Explain that this is critical for people to feel safe and trust the group and its members.

70 TWENTY QUESTIONS

In this engaging, fast-paced mixer, participants meet ten other participants and share information about personal stress and strategies for coping.

Goals

To get acquainted.

To share personal responses to stress and strategies for coping.

Materials

Worksheet: *Twenty Questions* (page 88)

Time Frame

10–15 minutes

Process

1. Distribute worksheets (adapted as needed to fit your group and themes). Explain that participants will have the opportunity to get acquainted with ten other people by playing Twenty Questions. Give directions for fast-paced, brief conversations in pairs.

   ■ Read over the questions, and add a few of your own that focus on _____ (your topic).

   ■ Pair up with someone you do not know and trade worksheets. Ask each other one question from the list and write your partner's answer in the space provided. You will have one minute to share and record answers.

   ■ When you hear the signal (whistle, horn, harmonica), it's your cue to find a new partner. Retrieve your worksheet; move on to a new partner, exchange worksheets with this person; and ask a new question from the list. Record each other's answers and when you hear the signal, move on to a third partner.

   ■ Keep moving from partner to partner, asking one question of each person, until you have talked to ten other participants.

2. Invite participants to share examples of what they learned from others or about themselves.

Variations

Create your own Twenty Questions worksheets to fit other topics, groups, and settings.

CONVERSATION STARTERS À LA CARTE

71 CAPTIONS

Props: ten Post-It Notes for each small group

In advance, cut out pictures from magazines portraying different health habits and life-style choices: images of athletes, people drinking beer and watching TV, families eating a healthy dinner, and so forth. Paste them on cardboard and hang them along a wall.

1. Form groups of three. Give each group several yellow sticky notes and tell them to roam through the gallery, look at the photos, write appropriate captions on the notes, and post them under the photos. The captions should express their feelings about the values underlying the images.

3. Reconvene the group and invite comments.

Variation: Choose images to fit the content of your presentation.

72 TABLE CONVERSATION

1. Assign people to groups with four or five members. Tell people to take turns talking for two minutes about a typical day, describing their energy flow, timing and pacing, high and low points, and the scheduling of "junk work."

2. After everyone has described a typical day, instruct small groups to discuss their ideas for coping with low points in the day. Allow four or five minutes. Interrupt and invite groups to share their best ideas with everyone.

73 BEST FRIENDS

1. Assign everyone to a small group and then instruct group members to introduce themselves by describing the personal qualities of their best childhood friend and their best adult friend. Each person has two minutes to share.

74 INSPIRATION SOURCES

1. Ask participants to reflect on personal sources of inspiration:

people or things that inspire them to do their best, be their best, cope with hard times, and keep trying to achieve their goals. Tell the group that sources of inspiration can be real or imagined, dead or alive, human or objects, works of art, scenes of nature, prayers, or even thoughts and feelings.

2. Form small groups and tell everyone to introduce themselves to their group and share one of their favorite sources of inspiration.

75 STAR TREK

1. Instruct participants to join a small group and introduce themselves by telling which planet, galaxy, or historical time period they would like to visit and why.

76 FAMILY TIME

1. Create small groups, and encourage participants to get acquainted by sharing information about how their family heated their home, celebrated birthdays, and spent Sunday nights when they were a child.

77 FAIRY TALES

1. Assign participants to small groups and then tell group members to go around the group and introduce themselves, sharing their favorite childhood story and telling why they liked it so much.

78 DISAPPOINTMENTS

1. Instruct participants to pair up with someone they do not know well. Ask them to describe disappointments that happened at three different points in their lives and explain how they handled them.

2. Encourage participants to discuss any new awareness or insights generated by sharing these experiences.

79 ADMIRABLE CHARACTERS

1. Divide people into small groups or pairs. Ask participants to name five people—dead or alive, real or imaginary—whom

they admire and to explain why they admire them.

2. Invite participants to share examples of admirable characters with the large group.

80 PRIZE POSSESSIONS

1. Assign people to small groups and then explain that each person has two minutes to tell the group about possessions they have that would mean little or nothing to someone else— but that they would not be able to part with easily.

81 GRADE SCHOOL

1. Form small groups. Invite people to take turns sharing a grade school experience they can still get back into emotionally. Explain that they should try to recall the feelings associated with this experience and tell the group about them.

2. Poll the large group as to which grade they were in at the time of their memorable incident.

82 AMUSING ANECDOTES

1. Have participants pair up with someone they do not know and tell about something funny that has happened to them.

2. Instruct participants to switch partners after two minutes and share a different amusing anecdote.

83 FAVORITE DESTINATION

1. Form groups with four to six members and ask people to introduce themselves by picking a place they have visited or would like to visit and explaining why they are attracted to this place.

2. After introductions, ask for examples of favorite destinations.

84 BINGO

1. Form small groups and instruct people to introduce them- selves as if they were playing a game of bingo, telling what they think their chances of winning would be and what their prize would be if they were to win.

85 PILLOW TALK / PILLOW FIGHT

1. Instruct group members to find a partner and then tell each other what issues they have been fighting about at home with a partner, kids, or other family members.

2. Next, ask everyone to tell their partners the kinds of things they say to other family members or to themselves before going to sleep.

86 PARABLES FOR LIFE

1. Read aloud to the group a touching parable, poem, or story.

2. Form groups of three or four and ask people to share examples of times when the message of the reading was (or would have been) inspiring in their lives.

87 FILM STAR

1. Ask participants to pair up with another group member and tell which actor or actress they would like to have play themselves in a film about their life, along with why they would choose this actor or actress.

88 MATCH UP

Props: Write thought-provoking quotations pertinent to the topic on three-by-five-inch index cards (one quote per card). Cut each card in half and put all card pieces in a basket.

1. As people enter the room, have each person draw a card and then find the person with the matching half of the quotation.

2. Once participants have found their partner, instruct pairs to take a five-minute walk and discuss their quote.

89 THE WAITING GAME

1. Assign everyone to a small group. Instruct group members to say their names, and complete the following sentence stubs:

   ▪ For me to be more creative, I'm waiting for . . .

   ▪ For me to be more healthy I'm waiting for . . .

2. Reconvene the group and survey members to identify some of the most common waiting games used by group members.

Variation: Create sentence stubs appropriate to your group and goals.

90 TELL ME

Worksheet: *Tell Me* (page 89)

1. Distribute worksheets. Invite participants to find a partner and sit down together.

2, When everyone is paired up, instruct people to ask each other one question from the list. Encourage participants to respond honestly, but make it clear that they may choose to pass if they don't want to answer a question. No one is to be made fun of for choosing to pass on a question. Tell participants they will have two minutes to exchange questions and answers.

2. Signal when it is time to switch partners and ask people to repeat the exchange, this time posing a different question to their new partner. Keep things moving along until people have talked with at least five others.

91 SHOPPING BAG

Worksheet: *Shopping Bag* (page 90)

1. Distribute worksheets and ask everyone to write down several of the tempting items they are likely to put in their cart when they go to the supermarket or discount store.

2. Direct participants to form a groups of four to six people and then introduce themselves by telling what is in their shopping bags and how they feel about buying these items.

Variation: substitute "things participants are shopping for in your workshop (or in their current job, etc.).

92 NAME CHANGE

1. Create groups of three and tell people to introduce themselves by first saying their name and then telling if they could change their name, to what they would change it and why.

Twenty Questions

1. How would you define stress?

2. What is one thing you do to reduce the harmful effects of stress?

3. Where in your body do you notice stress?

4. How do you reach to stress emotionally?

5. Where or how does stress manifest itself in your relationships?

6. How does stress affect your work?

7. What is one thing you do to reduce stress that ends up positive for you?

8. What is your biggest stressor at work?

9. What is your biggest stressor at home?

10. What are your strengths for coping with stress?

11. What is your number one negative way of handling stress?

12. What was stressful to you as a teenager that no longer causes you stress?

13. What connection do you make between stress and your values or spiritual dimension?

14. When do you get the most stressed out and what do you usually do about it?

15. What is the least stressful part of your work and why is it so stress-free?

16. In what ways do you create stress for the people around you?

17. Who is the best stress manager you know? Why does that person deserve the honor?

18.

19.

20.

Tell Me

One thing you hope to get from this gathering.

Some of the ways you like to be cared for.

What you look for in a friend.

Why you get up in the morning.

One way you need to take better care of yourself.

What motivated you to choose your job or profession.

One of your favorite ways to relax.

The bad habit you would like to break or give up.

Some favorite memories of your family as you were growing up.

If you could be a lobbyist in Congress for any cause, the issue you would speak up for and why.

One thing you particularly like about your job.

One thing that brought a smile to your face yesterday.

The peak time of the day for you when your energy is at its best.

Your favorite way to play.

What makes you special in your family or living group.

Your best self-care technique or habit.

One thing that makes you angry.

The most spiritually renewing thing you can do.

How you are most like others here.

How you are most different from others here.

Shopping Bag

TOOLS FOR SELF-AWARENESS

Paper-and-pencil tools are questionnaires or worksheets designed to evoke or facilitate individual reflection and comparisons with others in the group or the wide population. For many people, concrete data or results are compelling motivators for change.

GROUP DYNAMICS PRINCIPLES

Paper-and-pencil activities force participants to declare themselves in writing. To get something out of their head and onto paper and then to affirm it publicly is an enlightening process for many people who see themselves and their issues more clearly and definitively on paper than they do when they try to describe their experience verbally.

Self-awareness awakens self-responsibility. When people understand themselves, they can make conscious choices about what they want and need and how they will go about getting it. This empowers people to take initiative in a group and assume responsibility for their learning.

For kinesthetic learners, especially, the act of writing is a powerful learning modality. Kinesethetic learners use their body and their sense of touch to express things their mind knows but that they cannot express verbally. Drawing and writing can release body-mind wisdom.

Paper-and-pencil tools give shy people something to refer to when sharing. Many people find it easier to talk about themselves if they have something concrete to share: a score, a ranking on some scale, or a form completed. Paper tools provide structure for organizing personal experience and sharing with others.

Paper-and-pencil tools give the group a reference point for later discussions of problems and issues or resolutions and strategies. Participants can relate back to the instrument's content and use it as a focus or guide for reflection, discussion, problem-solving, planning, and follow-up. Take-home tools or instruments that can be repeated or applied to other situations empower participants to continue self-evaluation, rather than having to rely on group leaders or other experts for assessment.

Paper-and-pencil tools appeal to concrete thinkers. Some people

©1998 Whole Person Associates 210 W Michigan Duluth MN 55802   (800) 247-6789

want numbers rather than vague concepts to take home, for example, "I have eight of ten symptoms of stress, and 75 percent of people with this score suffer serious illness unless they practice relaxation or regular exercise five times a week." Concrete thinkers use numbers to reinforce personal motivation and set clear priorities for change.

TIPS FOR PLANNING AND IMPLEMENTATION

Allow time for getting acquainted before using paper-and-pencil tools. Because they involve silent, private reflection (followed by sharing), it's best to precede paper-and-pencil tools with an icebreaker that gets people talking to one another and sets the stage for an open, interactive group. Otherwise, a quiet, reflective process may backfire into a "no talking" rule that can inhibit group members from sharing experiences later.

Always provide time for public affirmation of what people discovered or learned. Give participants time to process their discoveries with a neighbor or small group and provide guidelines for sharing: Participants are in control of what they choose to share. People should listen without judging one another, or giving advice. Each person gets a fair share of time to talk.

Poll the group on scores or responses to key questions. This helps the leader get a feel for the group and allows group members to see how they compare to other participants. Polling the group also gives participants a comfortable way to risk disclosure, so they can discover that the group is a safe place, and it's okay to be different.

Make up your own instruments and continue to test and refine them with groups. Start with generalizations you've observed with groups, such as the common feelings of participants starting a new group, and transform these observations into a questionnaire or worksheet. Give it to participants and see what happens. After using what you learned to refine the instrument, give it to another group. When you make your own paper-and-pencil tools, you become authentically grounded in the material you present and bring integrity and power to your work.

Make up worksheets to fit your themes and the natural metaphors for groups, tasks, and issues. To get the creative juices flowing, try word associations to your theme or group, for example, police officer/badge, teacher/book, change/season. Then pick the best and design a worksheet around that idea. Unique, custom-designed worksheets add flair and pull your workshop together.

CAUTIONS

Before using paper-and-pencil tools, make sure they are appropriate and relevant for your group. Ask yourself: "Why am I doing this? Will it support my training design? Will it fit with participants' expectations? Am I allowing enough time to process it afterwards? Will it create unnecessary anxiety for participants? Thoughtful planning takes time in the beginning but saves time in the long run.

Don't get sidetracked by scoring controversies. Always provide a short time for clarification after you announce scoring. Explain that this is not a test like school, and there are no grades. Participants will figure their own score and decide what it means to them.

©1998 Whole Person Associates 210 W Michigan Duluth MN 55802   (800) 247-6789

93 AS WE BEGIN

In the beginning, participants analyze what they bring to the group—personal issues or concerns, specific wants and needs, motivation, attitude, and commitment—and decide how much responsibility they are willing to take in order to get what they want from the group.

Goals

To assess personal commitment and motivation for change.

To promote personal responsibility for learning and problem-solving within the group.

Time

10–15 minutes

Materials

Worksheet: *As We Begin* (page 100)

Process

1. Introduce the exercise by commenting on the responsibility people have for their own well-being and happiness and how the choices we make affect the quality of our day.

2. Hand out the worksheets and guide participants through a self-assessment of their issues, concerns, motivations, attitudes, and commitment.

   ■ On your worksheet, write what you specifically want from today, (e.g., to learn how to cope with stress).

   ■ Write specific ways to measure your satisfaction or success in reaching your goal (e.g., I'll have learned three new strategies for managing stress).

   ■ List what you are willing to do to get what you want (e.g., participate in the group, be honest, try one new thing).

   ■ Record one of the biggest problems, concerns, or issues that you bring to this learning experience (e.g., being over-whelmed by deadlines).

■ Write five personal guidelines for making today effective (e.g., keep an open mind, don't jump to conclusions, think before speaking).

■ On a scale of one to ten, with one representing very low commitment and ten representing very high, what is your current commitment to the personal goals and responsibilities you've identified?

■ Write your current commitment score on your worksheet.

3. Form groups of three or four people and ask everyone to share their assessments.

■ Starting with the person who traveled the farthest to get here today, take two minutes each to share as much as you want about your issues, attitudes, motivations, and commitment.

■ The person to the right of the speaker is timekeeper.

4. Reconvene the group and poll members about their responses to key questions. Summarize common issues, goals, and guidelines for making the day more effective.

Variation

Change the wording on the worksheet and offer a second, closing exercise, calling it *As We Conclude*. Have participants review or evaluate how the day went, whether they got what they wanted, and whether they assumed responsibility for their learning goals.

PAPER & PENCIL TOOLS À LA CARTE

94 TOOL BELT

Worksheet: *Tool Belt* (page 101)

1. Distribute worksheets and ask participants to assess the tools they have for coping with stress and taking care of themselves. Tell everyone to write (or draw) all their tools on the worksheet, adding as many as they can think of to their belt.

2. Instruct participants to form groups of four and show or describe to other group members their tools for self-care.

3. Poll the group for examples of resources used by members.

Variation: Focus on tools that fit the agenda of your group (e.g., time management, creativity, team-building).

95 WHOLE-PERSON PACIFIER

Props: baby's pacifier
Worksheet: *Whole-Person Pacifier* (page 102)

1. Hold the pacifier and talk about the importance of adult, whole-person pacifiers—strategies or activities that give comfort and nurture each individual's physical, emotional, mental, spiritual, interpersonal, and career needs.

2. Hand out worksheets and ask participants to identify their whole-person pacifiers, writing one example for each area of self-care on their worksheet.

3. Tell participants to pair up and share their pacifiers, explaining to their partner what they are and when they are used.

96 BRIEF HEALTH ASSESSMENT

Materials: blank paper

1. Distribute paper and tell participants to fold their paper in half vertically, forming two columns. They should write "What I've Been Doing That's Healthful" at the top of the left column, and "What I've Been Doing That's Harmful" at the top of the right column.

2. Tell everyone to be as honest as they can as they write down all

the healthful and harmful things they have been doing this year.

3. Ask people to pair up and discuss the results of their brief health assessment.

Variation: Adapt the assessment to fit your needs (e.g., "What I've been doing that helps or hurts the team").

97 LIKERT SCALE: HEALTH BELIEFS

Worksheet: *Health Beliefs* (page 103)

1. Distribute worksheets and ask participants to examine their personal beliefs about health by circling the response that most closely describes the degree to which they believe each statement. (The "strongly agree" to "strongly disagree" designation is called a Likert scale.)

2. Form small groups and tell participants to take turns sharing their strongest (strongly agree and strongly disagree) beliefs with the group.

3. Invite individuals or small groups to share examples of their strongest beliefs with the large group.

Variation: Rewrite the belief statements to fit the topic of concern to your group.

98 STRESS GRID

Worksheet: *Stress Grid* (page 104)

1. Briefly explain four sources of stress: catastrophic events, (life-threatening, natural disasters, assaults), major life events (birth, death, marriage, divorce), minor life events (daily hassles that can be cumulative or chronic), and personal or low self-esteem stress (when low self-esteem creates pervasive anxiety and stress).

2. Distribute worksheets and ask people to plot their personal stress grid by putting a check mark beside the types and sources of stress they experienced over the past three to six months.

3. Ask participants to find a partner and share the patterns displayed on their grids.

99 ATTITUDE CHECKUP

Materials: blank paper

1. Distribute paper and ask participants to do a quick attitude checkup by answering three questions, using a scale from one to ten (1=not at all, 10=extremely):

   - How interested are you in learning about the topic?
   - How willing are you to look at yourself?
   - How willing are you to talk about yourself?

2. Tell participants to compute their score by adding the three rankings for a total score, then explain how to interpret these scores:

1–15	It might be better to go shopping.
16–24	You'll get something out of the workshop.
25–30	You'll have a life-changing day.

3. Instruct participants to form triads and brainstorm for two minutes on possible strategies for raising their attitude scores.

100 ON HOLD

Materials: blank paper

1. Distribute paper and ask participants to make a list of the things they have been putting off or on putting on hold until some aspect of themselves is different, for example, until they lose weight, exercise, understand a new job, or go back to school.

2. Form groups of three or four people. Ask members to tell one thing they have been putting on hold and discuss specific things they could do right now to enable themselves to act.

3. Invite group members to share with the entire group examples of things they have put on hold and strategies for acting now.

101 SPIRITUAL WELLNESS

Worksheet: *Spiritual Wellness* (page 105)

1. Introduce spiritual wellness as an important, but often overlooked, component of life-style wellness, and invite partici-

pants to assess their spiritual wellness or ability to have faith, hope, and love.

2. Hand out worksheets and ask people to assess their spiritual wellness on a continuum from one to ten.

3. Choose one of the questions and instruct participants to stand and make a human continuum, based on their ranking for that item, from one side of the room to the other. Invite them to pair up with someone close to them on the continuum to share discoveries about their spiritual wellness.

Variation: Develop a similar list of position statements on your topic and use the same process.

102 EMOTIONAL MATURITY SCALE

Worksheet: *Emotional Maturity Scale* (page 106)

1. Give each person a worksheet and ask them to evaluate their emotional maturity on a scale from one to ten, with ten being the most mature possible.

2. Ask people to put a star beside the area in which they are the most mature and a circle around the area in which they are least mature.

3. Divide the group into triads and tell participants to take turns sharing their maturity scale scores, telling one way they want to become more emotionally mature and suggesting one idea for moving in that direction.

As We Begin

I am responsible for what I learn.

What I want specifically from today is _____

_____

I'll know I'll have reached that goal when _____

_____

In order to get what I want today, I am willing to _____

_____

One of the biggest problems, issues or concerns I bring to this learning experience is _____

_____

I am responsible to be an active learner, searching for strategies that will help transform this problem, issue, or concern into an opportunity for growth and change.

Guidelines to make this learning experience more effective

1. _____
2. _____
3. _____
4. _____
5. _____

On a scale from 1 to 10, right now I am a _____

©1998 Whole Person Associates 210 W Michigan Duluth MN 55802 (800) 247-6789

Tool Belt

Fill the space around the tool belt with words or pictures depicting your personal tools and resources.

Whole Person Pacifiers

	What are they?	When do you use them?
Physical	_____	_____
	_____	_____
	_____	_____
Emotional	_____	_____
	_____	_____
	_____	_____
Spiritual	_____	_____
	_____	_____
	_____	_____
Mental	_____	_____
	_____	_____
	_____	_____
Interpersonal	_____	_____
	_____	_____
	_____	_____
Career/job	_____	_____
	_____	_____
	_____	_____

Health Beliefs

	SD	D	N/O	A	SA
The rights of nonsmokers are equal to those of smokers.					
Two drinks of alcohol per day. will prolong my life.					
People can (I can) control health.					
Disease is my fault.					
Wellness will add years to life.					
Giving to others is part of being well.					
Most Americans are malnourished.					
Good health comes from good genes.					
Being alone/lonely doesn't affect health.					
Relaxation costs money.					
An apple a day keeps the doctor away.					
Poor people are at greater risk for illness.					
Positive attitude affects health.					
Pollution is not my responsibility.					

Stress Grid

Types of Stressors	Catastrophic	Major Life	Minor Life	Personal
Personal				
Emotional				
Physical				
Mental				
Spiritual				
Pain				
Disease				
Commuting				
Change				
Financial				
Interpersonal				
Marital/Family				
Social				
Work/Recreation				
Job				
Unemployment				
Leisure Activities				
Ecological				
Environmental				
Chemical				

Spiritual Wellness

Rank yourself on a scale from 1–10 for each dimension of spiritual wellness.

_____   I have a *mission or purpose* in life.

_____   God or a Higher Power has *priority* in my daily life and leisure time.

_ _____   I express *care and concern* for others.

_____   I *intercede* on behalf of others, seek agreement.

_____   I seek God's (or Higher Power's) *purpose* in my life.

_____   I judge myself, but *I don't judge others* for their mistakes.

_____   I am *trustworthy and reliable* with others.

_____   I am *responsible and responsive* in giving and receiving love.

_____   *Prayer and worship* are priorities in my life.

_____   My *standard of living* matches my expectations of others.

_____   I experience *happiness and peace.*

Emotional Maturity Scale

Able to deal constructively with reality

I _____ 1 0

Able to adapt to change

I _____ 1 0

Free from symptoms produced by tension and anxiety

I _____ 1 0

Able to find more satisfaction in giving than receiving

I _____ 1 0

Able to relate to other people in a consistent manner
with mutual satisfaction and helpfulness

I _____ 1 0

Able to sublimate, to direct my instinctive hostile energy
into creative and constructive outlets

I _____ 1 0

Able to love

I _____ 1 0

Attributed to William C. Menninger, MD

©1998 Whole Person Associates 210 W Michigan Duluth MN 55802   (800) 247-6789

DISCUSSIONS & BRAINSTORMING

Although we take discussions and brainstorming for granted, they are powerful tools for generating ideas, sharing experience, building understanding, solving problems, stimulating creativity, heightening involvement, and building teamwork. Even gifted teachers and trainers may underutilize this valuable learning modality if they don't consciously focus on creating time and employing strategies that intentionally generate ideas and stimulate discussion.

GROUP DYNAMICS PRINCIPLES

Discussions increase participation. When everyone's ideas are valued, and it is clear that nobody's ideas will be censored or criticized, people who are normally quiet, shy, or passive are encouraged to express themselves vigorously. This is a confidence-builder because people discover not only that it is safe to express ideas—it's also fun. As people start to enjoy the process, they participate more spontaneously, and their commitment goes up.

Participation promotes teamwork. Brainstorming, discussions, and consensus decision-making promote a sense of ownership by the group for ideas generated and issues raised. Usually a group-building rapport results, and the group experiences success in completing its task.

Group brainstorming builds powerful synergy. More ideas, solutions, information, and facts can be generated by groups than by individuals alone. Not only can groups germinate more ideas than individuals, they can do it in a shorter time. Information sprouted in a group is more likely to be accurate and to be retained by group members. When group synergy wells up, participants are launched into powerful learning experiences.

Discussions pool the collective wisdom of the group. Participants have much to learn from and to teach each other. When individuals share life experience and creative energy with others, they start a learning momentum that ripples throughout the entire group and benefits everyone.

The best way to have good ideas is to have lots of ideas. The more data people have, the better the decisions they make. Brainstorming gives people more data, fast.

Discussions provide valuable "air time." Saying something out loud is powerful. Sometimes people surprise themselves with what they state—a personal truth, belief, or feeling that runs more deeply than they thought and which, once declared, becomes a clear focal point for learning, problem-solving, and personal change.

TIPS FOR PLANNING & IMPLEMENTATION

Give clear instructions so groups know the task and time frame. Explain that the purpose of brainstorming is to break out of old thinking, generate as many ideas as possible in a short time, and allow everyone air time. Be specific about what people are to focus on, how ideas are to be recorded, what they are to do with the information, and how much time they have to complete the task.

For discussions, provide structure that promotes participation. Explain rules for taking turns, timekeeping, order, and the preliminary individual reflection that may precede sharing with the group. Structure ensures that all group members have a chance to participate.

For discussions, allow time for all to participate. Allow enough time for everyone to speak up or become engaged, but always call a halt while energy is still high, rather than waiting for groups to wind down. Because there are always unexpected developments or delays, plan extra time in case you need it. Clear but flexible time limits are best.

Set clear ground rules. Before any small group activity, state the ground rules or have participants brainstorm their own by responding to the question: What do you need from the group members and leader to participate fully and feel safe with the group? Common responses are confidentiality, no judgments or put-downs, affirmation that all ideas are valuable, careful listening, and an equal chance to speak. When expectations are clearly stated and consciously agreed upon, people are more likely to move ahead with eagerness and commitment.

For maximum involvement, create groups of three to six members. Don't try a discussion with more than six or eight people. Since there is not enough time for larger groups to allow each person to speak, what often happens is that natural leaders and extroverts do all or most of the talking, while followers and introverts sit quietly and may feel powerless, frustrated, or bored. Smaller groups provide time in the spotlight for everyone, which affirms each person for participating and builds group intimacy.

For brainstorming, focus on a single problem or issue. Don't skip to various problems or try to brainstorm complex issues. The opportunity to delve into one problem or issue at a time allows group members to channel creative energy into immediate, comprehensive responses to the problem or issue at hand.

Change groups often so different viewpoints and perspectives are available to all. Participants have a lot to offer one another, so the more people have an opportunity to talk with folks whose perspective or life experience may be different from their own, the better. Diversity enriches the group; fresh perspectives are a gift.

Brainstorming and consensus decision-making make problem-solving fun and stimulating each step of the way. When groups engage in problem-solving, they follow a stimulating process: 1) define the problem or issue, 2) brainstorm solutions to the problem or issue (including wild, crazy ideas), 3) review, change, and prioritize ideas, and 4) adopt the best one by consensus, which means that most people agree, and there is no strong opposition to the group decision. Not only is this method of problem-solving and decision-making fun, it's effective.

CAUTIONS

Some people need more time for thinking and processing before producing. Others are reluctant to speak up in a group. Deal with potential roadblocks by providing time for individual reflection before a group activity and by drawing out silent members.

Circulate and watch for groups where highly verbal folks are dominating. Encourage shy people to speak up. Ask at the end for anyone who hasn't spoken yet to add a comment. Periodically mix up groups so no one gets stuck with an unproductive combination for long.

Some groups take longer to warm up to brainstorming. If you see the group struggling to think of ideas, prime the pump with examples to get the creative juices flowing. Offer a few outrageous, funny ideas. Be a role model for flexible thinking, and encourage participants to not take the task—or themselves—too seriously.

Guarded, restricted communication usually indicates low group trust. You may need to spend more time getting acquainted or doing group-building activities. If you've tried this, and people still seem to be holding back, you can ask the group for feedback: is there a problem with trust or have you missed something in planning group activities? Chances are good that someone will be honest and tell you what's going on.

103 PROGRESS REPORT

By keeping a running list of ideas for how to use, modify, adapt, and apply what they've learned so far, participants keep track of their progress and mobilize the resources of the group.

Goals

To cultivate the resources of the group, and augment learning.

Time

5–10 minutes

Materials

White board or newsprint and easel, markers

Process

This process is best suited for longer workshops.

1. After a period of concentrated study or exploration, ask participants to enlarge their range of learning by creating a running list of ideas for how to use, modify, adapt, and apply what they have learned so far.

   ■ Grab two other people and form a trio.

   ■ Brainstorm ideas for how you could use the techniques you've learned so far.

   ■ Think of ways to modify, adapt, apply, stretch, and integrate the ideas into your current life situation. Look for a whole range of divergent ideas.

   ■ The shortest person writes down all ideas and reports back to the large group.

   ■ Think of as many ideas as you can in three minutes.

2. Signal time to stop brainstorming, and start a progress report on a white board or newsprint, listing all ideas generated by small groups. Praise the group for their ingenuity and then announce that you will conduct another progress report later in the session.

3. Repeat progress report activity at least once more, adding to the running list and reviewing ideas previously cultivated as you go.

DISCUSSION & BRAINSTORMING À LA CARTE

104 ANONYMOUS BRAINSTORMING

Materials: three-by-five-inch index cards

1. Create several small groups. Give each small group a stack of index cards and instruct participants to brainstorm solutions to a specific issue or problem, writing ideas anonymously, one idea per card.

2. Collect all the cards. Read them aloud and tack them on a board as you read them. Try grouping cards or ideas according to general themes. Affirm participants for their great ideas and carry on with the next activity, weaving the ideas into subsequent discussions.

105 FORCE FIT

Materials: poster board for each small group, markers

1. Create groups of four to six people. Give each group a sheet of poster board and a word or phrase that seems unrelated to your topic (for example, world hunger, sexual harassment, party 'til you drop). Tell people to brainstorm what this word or phrase has to do with the topic of the day. They should make a poster representing these ideas and report back to the large group.

2. Lead small groups in poster presentations to the large group and then hang or display posters around the room.

106 QUESTIONS AND ANSWERS

1. After a full-length presentation or group learning activity, tell participants to pair up with someone and have a private question-and-answer session, making up probing questions and answers related to topics or issues discussed in the group.

2. Reconvene the large group and invite participants to share their questions anonymously, using "we" rather than revealing which person said what.

107 RANKING

Materials: In advance, make up ranking sheets with several groupings of three or four choices, all of which are likely to be appealing or unappealing to participants (for example, after a busy day, how would you prefer to relax: active exercise, a drink or two, watch TV, talk to spouse/friend/family member?).

1. Distribute sheets and ask participants to arrange the choices in order of their preference, ranking their first choice as one, their second as two, and so forth.

2. Create groups with three or four members, including some who agree on rankings and some who disagree. Ask people to take turns explaining or defending their rankings to the group while others listen without judging. Each person has two minutes to talk.

108 DEFINITIONS

1. Ask each person to write a definition of self-esteem and then join a group of three or four people to share personal definitions.

2. Ask volunteers to share their definitions with the large group and then direct the groups to discuss how self-esteem can be achieved regardless of personal flaws.

3. Invite each group to share their ideas with the large group.

Variation: Choose a word for definition appropriate to your learning objectives.

109 BRIGHT IDEAS

Worksheet: *Bright Ideas* (page 116)

1. Identify a problem or issue on which to focus. Give each person a worksheet and ask people to brainstorm as many ideas or solutions to the problem as they can in two minutes, writing all ideas—even crazy or impractical ones—on their light bulb.

2. Invite participants to take turns sharing their enlightenment with a small group or the large group, encouraging others to note potentially useful ideas or solutions.

Variation: Create small groups first and make a group idea list.

110 TAKE 5

1. Create groups with five members. Ask participants to brainstorm ideas for five-minute break activities that will nourish, replenish, or energize their small group.

2. Tell each small group to select their favorite idea by voting and then "take 5" and do it.

3. After five minutes, reconvene the group and ask members to share their "take 5" experiences.

111 CAN OF SQUIRMS

Materials: In preparation, make a can of squirms by writing a variety of topics or words on three-by-five-inch index cards (one topic or word per card) and distributing the cards into several large coffee cans.

1. Create small groups. Give each group a can of squirms and instruct group members to take turns pulling out a card and giving an impromptu, two-minute speech on what that idea or word has to do with the day's topic. Individuals can pass or draw another card, but everyone should say something.

112 PLAY BALL

Props: tennis or beach ball for each small group

1. Identify a topic to be brainstormed and create small groups. Instruct participants in each group to stand or sit in a circle facing the center. Give a ball to one person in each group and explain that people holding the ball are to say the first thing that enters their mind on the identified topic and then toss the ball to another group member.

2. The process continues as participants catch the ball, share the first thing that enters their mind on the topic, and then toss the ball to someone else.

3. Stop the game after everyone has had a chance to contribute. Solicit examples of brainstormed ideas from the large group.

113 ADVANTAGES

Materials: blank paper

1. Distribute paper and tell participants to think of one undesirable quality they have. Working individually, people should brainstorm the advantages of being a person with that quality, listing every possible advantage they can think of—no matter how trivial.

2. Form triads and ask group members to discuss the advantages of having the flaws they identified. Instruct people to add to their list advantages suggested by the other two.

3. Solicit from each group examples of advantages to having certain undesirable qualities.

©1998 Whole Person Associates 210 W Michigan Duluth MN 55802   (800) 247-6789

Bright Ideas

ANALOGIES & METAPHORS

Analogies and metaphors are intriguing tools for engaging participants in nonlinear thinking. They give everyone the opportunity to practice seeing things from many different perspectives. This modeling of open-mindedness sets the stage for creativity and problem-solving. When people are invited to make creative comparisons, they often discover new insights and forms of self-expression. When the process is shared in a group, perceptions of self and others can be dramatically transformed.

GROUP DYNAMICS PRINCIPLES

Analogies and metaphors are powerful learning tools. Creating analogies and metaphors is like adding a wide-angle or close-up lens to your camera; suddenly you see your environment from a whole new perspective. New information comes into awareness—information taken from one context and applied to another—resulting in creativity, flexibility, and innovative problem-solving.

Analogies enhance group learning and individual potency. Each person's metaphor is different and valuable. Sharing unique perceptions reinforces the idea that group members can learn from each other.

Analogies and metaphors give structure for novel self-reflection. Inventing analogies and metaphors requires that participants think of themselves and others in a totally new way, identifying with objects, events, or phrases not normally used to describe personal experience. What emerges, for individuals and for the group itself, is often striking in its clarity and meaning.

Metaphors universalize group members' experiences. Force-fit analogies provide common denominators for group members. For example, if everyone has to describe their current life-style with a song title, musical analogies become a universal theme for the group. Universality is a key factor in building group cohesion.

Analogies build trust and intimacy. Because personally chosen metaphors are so striking and meaningful for participants, they evoke empathy, compassion, and understanding between group members.

Some analogies are funny; others may be sad or touching, sometimes moving people to tears. When people share with this level of openness, trust is born, and intimacy follows.

TIPS FOR PLANNING AND IMPLEMENTATION

Provide gender-neutral or gender-mixed objects or themes. Select objects or themes everyone can identify with, such as animals, birds, food, music, sports, weather, plants, and colors. As an extra precaution, ask a friend or colleague for feedback on the gender-neutrality of selected objects and themes.

Consider the level of risk or self-disclosure most appropriate for your group. High-risk analogies and metaphors about family relationships or personal problems elicit more self-disclosure, more emotion, and more group intensity. While this may be appropriate for ongoing growth or counseling groups, it is not appropriate for most educational groups or workshops.

Provide for the seven ways of knowing. Because people learn in seven different ways, include analogies and metaphors from each of these areas: visual/spatial, musical/rhythmic, logical/mathematical, body/kinesthetic, verbal/linguistic, interpersonal, and intrapersonal.

Include specific issues, team concerns and current situations as objects of metaphor. You'll learn a lot about people and their situations, and you may discover opportunities for problem solving in the process. Illustrate your general metaphor with specific examples. If you ask people to describe themselves as a type of book, suggest mystery, romance, biography, autobiography, travel guides, historical fiction, cookbooks, prayer books, references, poetry, and art and picture books.

Brainstorm a list of objects that can be used as analogies or metaphors. For each object, develop a list of possible examples. They'll come in handy in case participants need help priming the pump.

Create your own analogy and metaphor worksheets. Use sentence completions appropriate to your group, topic, and setting. For example:

- If I were a _____ (food), I would be _____ .
- My coping style is most like a _____ (type of bird).
- My learning style is most like a _____ (animal).

- My approach to conflict resembles _____ (weather pattern).
- My attitude toward this change sounds like _____ (type of music).

CAUTIONS

Some people have a hard time with imaginary tasks or playing with words. Offer several concrete, specific, graphic options that will be familiar to your audience. For example, display several cartoons and ask people to identify which one is most like their current situation. With a more open-ended task, give several examples: Is this change more like a football game, a fencing match, a relay race, or a marathon?

Analogies and metaphors sometimes elicit strong emotions. Occasionally, an analogy or metaphor will trigger painful emotions. An old grief may surface; tears may flow. Be prepared to offer support, time for further processing, and referral to a professional counselor if needed.

114 PICTURE POSTCARDS

Identification with images or picture postcards provides vivid introductions in groups of all sizes and types.

Goals

To get acquainted.

To facilitate self-disclosure and initial bonding.

Materials

Unused picture postcards (at least 20 percent more than the number of people expected). Postcards could be grouped thematically (e.g., local scenery, landmarks, animals, plants, birds, skylines from cities around the world, scenes of natural beauty, art reproductions, maps, humorous images). Build up a collection as you travel or swap cards with friends in other areas to add diversity to the local fare. Expect some postcards to disappear each time you use this exercise. People tend to get attached to their chosen image.

Process

1. Select postcards to suit your group and objectives.
2. Spread the postcards on a large table, creating a gallery that is easily viewed by participants.
3. Invite people to visit the gallery.
   - Take a minute to view the collection of images in the gallery, paying special attention to any that intrigue you.
   - Select one postcard that you identify with and take it with you as you return to your seat.
3. When everyone has a card, proceed with introductions.
   - Introduce yourself to the group, stating your name and telling why you chose this particular postcard and how it represents you or your life.

Variations

- Divide into small groups for introductions. Use a theme to match your postcards (e.g., trios born in the same—or different—states or cities, quartets who have visited—or would like to visit—popular locations, such as Disneyland, the Statue of Liberty, etc.).

- As a closing exercise, especially appropriate for ongoing groups, have participants select a card from the gallery as a symbolic gift or wish for another group member. Allow them to share their gifts in small groups. Start by sharing one of the cards you chose, explaining why you selected it, for example, "I chose this picture of a woman walking on the beach because I think you long for solitude and quiet in your life, and my wish for you is that you find it."

ANALOGIES & METAPHORS À LA CARTE

115 ENERGY THERMOMETER

Worksheet: *Thermometer* (page 128)

1. Distribute worksheets and introduce the metaphor of an energy thermometer, a subjective measurement of each participant's current energy level.

2. Each person decides how high or low their current energy level would be on the thermometer and uses a colored marker or crayon to shade in the mercury to that level.

3. In pairs, people share energy thermometers and the reasons for current readings.

Variation: Use the thermometer for assessing commitment level, enthusiasm, course evaluation, or any other dynamic.

116 ZOO TIME

1. What animal best describes your usual style of stress management, conflict resolution, or time management?

2. Introduce yourself telling about your animal analogy.

117 YEARBOOK

Materials: blank paper and markers

1. Distribute paper and markers. Invite people to imagine that this is their yearbook page for the past year and to write a self-description that includes accomplishments, activities, and qualities.

2. Think of three other people who might write in your yearbook: a close friend or buddy, a casual acquaintance, and someone from your family. Write notes to yourself from each of these people. If you want, add notes from people at work.

3. Find three people who did not graduate from high school within three years of you. Introduce yourselves and share yearbook entries.

118 AUTHORS

1. Ask participants to imagine themselves as authors and create a book title based on a specific topic or issue.
2. They should complete the sentence: If I wrote a book today, its title would be _____.
3. They should then introduce themselves as authors, sharing book titles and backgrounds with the group.

119 SELF SYMBOL

Materials: blank paper and pens, crayons, or markers

1. Draw a symbol of yourself on a piece of paper.
2. Introduce yourself, explaining your symbol verbally or demonstrating its meaning nonverbally.

120 AUTO PARTS

1. Pair up with someone who drives a different make of car than you drive.
2. Select the part of a car that best describes you and tell your partner what it is and why you chose this part.

121 BELTS AND BUCKLES

Materials: construction paper or poster board and markers or crayons

1. Distribute art materials and ask people to design a personal belt and buckle.

   ■ Model it after tooled belts with names carved in the leather and fancy, meaningful belt buckles.

   ■ Put your name on the outside of the belt.

   ■ Design a buckle showing your greatest accomplishment.

   ■ Besides holding up your jeans, belts can also hold in feelings. Write on the inside of your belt feelings you don't show to others.

2. Form groups of six or eight people based on the color or type of garments people are wearing., Invite participants to

©1998 Whole Person Associates 210 W Michigan Duluth MN 55802   (800) 247-6789

introduce themselves by showing their belts and sharing some of their hidden feelings.

3. When everyone has been introduced, link all the belts together and hang them in the room.

122 GALLERY TOUR

Materials: Before your session, cut out pictures from newspapers or magazines that could communicate something about the issues you will be addressing. Paste these images on construction paper, one image per sheet. Make more than enough for the number of people you expect.

1. Post the mounted pictures on the wall or spread them on a table and invite people to choose the image that most attracts them. With large groups leave the pictures hanging in the gallery and ask participants to view them all and then make their selection by number or description.

2. In pairs, trios, or small groups, let people briefly describe their connection to the picture and how it might relate to the group's theme.

Variation: Small groups could choose an image to represent their team and create a caption for their group picture.

123 HEROES AND HEROINES

Worksheet: Heroes and Heroines (page 129)

1. Distribute worksheets and give instructions for reflection, adapting them to your topics and issues.

   ■ At the top list five people, dead or alive, whom you admire and briefly note why.

   ■ Choose one person from the list. In what ways are you similar to this person? Write the similarities in space A.

   ■ In space B, write some ways you are like this person in relation to the group's topic.

   ■ In space C, write how you are similar to this person in relation to another aspect of the group's topic.

2. Ask participants to tell a partner about their heroes and

heroines, focusing particularly on the traits they have in common with these admired models.

124 TRACK MEET

1. Compare your stress management style (or interpersonal or problem-solving style) to a track and field event or participant: 100 yard dash, mile relay, high hurdles, low hurdles, steeple chase, pole vault, triple jump, broad jump, decathlon, mile run, marathon, shot-put, javelin, discus, spectator, timekeeper, announcer, coach, judge/official, concession stand, groundskeeper.

2. Introduce yourself to the group, using the track meet metaphor to describe your stress management style.

Variation: Apply the track meet metaphor to an issue appropriate to your group and educational goals (e.g., interpersonal style, management style, problem-solving approach, conflict management).

125 IF I WERE . . .

Props: In advance, write a list of nouns on a whiteboard or newsprint (e.g., tree, bird, dog, weather, song, dance, art work, season, color, beverage, road, house, automobile, book, toy, car, body of water, piece of furniture).

1. Starting at the top of the list, participants create a personal analogy to the designated noun and use it to introduce themselves, briefly explaining the meaning of the analogy. For example, "If I were a tree, I'd be an oak because I'm tall and sturdy, good at weathering storms."

3. If time allows, do several round robins, using different words and personal analogies.

126 VICE GRIP

Worksheet: *Vice Grip* (page 130)

1. Distribute worksheets and ask participants to identify stressors that squeeze them. These may be habits, pressures, deadlines, or attitudes that are self-defeating or limit options.

©1998 Whole Person Associates 210 W Michigan Duluth MN 55802   (800) 247-6789

2. Ask people to share their "gripping" stress stories with a partner or small group.

Variation: Brainstorm ideas for loosening the squeeze of the vice grip and pursuing healthy relief from stress.

127 WATERING CAN

Worksheet: Watering Can (page 131)

1. Distribute worksheets and ask participants to think about the parched areas of their life, the areas in need of watering.

- What do you need sprinkled over your life?
- What are you thirsty for?
- What aspect of your life do you want to grow?
- Write reflections on your worksheet.

2. Share in pairs or small groups.

128 MATH AND SCIENCE

1. Introduce yourself as a math concept, biological concept, chemical reaction, simple machine, endangered species, or engineering principle.

2. Tell about yourself and your chosen math or science analogy.

129 COLORFUL CHARACTERS

1. Direct participants to introduce themselves as a color and then listen as others in their small group tell about their favorite objects in that color.

130 TASTEFUL INTRODUCTIONS

1. Ask people to pair up with another person and introduce themselves as a type of food, briefly explaining why they identify with this particular type of food.

2. Each pair should then join with three other pairs, to form a group of eight people. Partners now introduce each other by the food they have chosen to identify with, sharing their partner's reasons for picking this food.

131 SECRET METAPHORS

Materials: small slips of paper, bowl or hat (one for each small group)

1. Distribute slips of paper and ask participants to write on them the name of the musical instrument that best conveys their personality. They should then fold the paper and put it in the hat or bowl in the center of the group.

2. Draw a paper out of the hat and read the musical instrument written on it. Then ask participants to guess which group member picked that instrument. When the identity of the person is revealed, she briefly shares how or why she is like that instrument. Then another slip of paper is drawn, and the guessing continues until all participants have been identified.

Variation: In groups larger than 10–12, divide into small groups for guessing and introduction.

132 FLEA MARKET

Materials: In advance, collect a box of assorted junk items (e.g., craft materials, rubber stamps, paper, photos, ribbon, an old shoe, gum, pop, rubber bands, string, books, dolls, games, toys, small tools, kitchen gadgets).

1. Spread the flea market objects out on a long table, and ask participants to silently view the objects, select one that they identify with, and return to their seat.

2. Form small groups based on street addresses (e.g., ends in an odd or even number, ends in 1–3, 4–6, 7–0—whatever will result in groups of 5–8 folks). People take turns introducing themselves using their chosen flea market find, telling what it represents and why they selected it.

©1998 Whole Person Associates 210 W Michigan Duluth MN 55802   (800) 247-6789

Thermometer

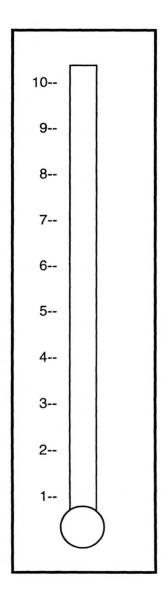

Heroes and Heroines

1 _____

2. _____

3. _____

4. _____

5. _____

A. Ways in which I am similar to my hero.

B. Ways in which I am like my hero in connection with an aspect of our group's topic for today.

C. Ways in which I am like my hero in connection with another aspect of our topic.

Vice Grip

Watering Can

CREATIVE ACTIVITIES

Creative activities are especially appropriate for workshops and ongoing groups. Even though they take more time than quick icebreakers or paper-and-pencil tools, creative activities are worth including in any educational experience. Creativity makes groups come alive: energy becomes charged; insights are discovered; and group bonding deepens.

GROUP DYNAMICS PRINCIPLES

Creativity is the wellspring of all functional groups. Regardless of the group's purpose, the heart of all groups is creative synergy, the process that invites something new to come into existence. Creativity brings tangible and intangible benefits: visible rewards like clever business logos, inspiring mission statements, and exciting new products; invisible treasures such as renewed energy, commitment, hope, laughter, self-awareness, and teamwork. Creativity is the spark that makes it all happen.

Creative activities liberate right-brain wisdom. Too often, our work and training ask us to think and be logical, not to explore feelings or be spontaneous and playful. Yet thinking in images as well as words captures feelings and attitudes that conventional, left-brain reasoning cannot. Painting a picture, singing a song, or solving a puzzle unleashes childlike curiosity, intuition, humor, and impetuousness, which is refreshing, original, and often enlightening.

Artistic activities can lower defenses. Since artistic activities approach the self through a new perspective and unfamiliar medium, psychological and perceptual defenses are lowered. Any creation is "right"; uniqueness is valued; and it's okay to be different. Having a choice in the type of self-expression and level of self-disclosure makes participants feel safe, not threatened. This helps people relax and open up.

Creativity is often a group leveler. Nonverbal folks may shine at something else, like drawing, writing, or acting. This not only equalizes power and status, it also highlights hidden resources of group members. When these talents are recognized and utilized, the entire group benefits.

People have different learning styles. While some people learn easily by listening to a speaker and taking notes, others learn best (or get ready to learn) by engaging in nontraditional styles of learning, such as movement or listening to music. Providing a variety of methods is best because it takes into account the differing learning styles of participants.

Experiences go to a deeper level and more quickly without words. Sculpting an object or symbol in clay quickly taps into depths that are not easily captured in words. Discovery of unspoken meanings, feelings, and attitudes is powerful; such insights bring self-awareness and personal growth.

Shared creative activity provides a powerful group bond. Having a deeper focus and increased self-awareness changes the way people communicate with others; feelings and attitudes are expressed openly and authentically, resulting in increased understanding of others. With few exceptions, these tender shoots of empathy grow into a garden of meaningful connections between group members.

Creative activities accelerate learning. When playful, childlike qualities of adults are set free, people are open to new experiences, and willing to try new things. Novelty arouses interest and makes learning fun. As people share individual or group creativity, they demonstrate novel problem-solving methods, which helps others learn by example. And creative, dramatic activities offer a change of pace, which all groups need to keep energy and learning at a peak.

Artistic expression builds pride. Individuals and groups feel pride in personal accomplishments, in being able to say, "I made this painting," or "we created this skit." It's satisfying and fun to make something unique, and share results with an appreciative audience.

Music can set a mood for group activity. Playing music from the sound track of *Chariots of Fire* will create an inspiring, high-charged atmosphere for creative problem-solving. Soft, classical music enhances personal reflection and imagery; while loud, silly songs create a lighthearted mood. Music will always stimulate a mood; when selected carefully, it will not detract from learning but will enhance it.

TIPS FOR PLANNING AND IMPLEMENTATION

Create an atmosphere that rewards creativity and discourages negativity. Reward creativity by reinforcing creative expression when it happens. Praise participants who volunteer original ideas, take risks, or try new things. Discourage negative comments, criticism, and argumentation. Most important, be genuinely enthusiastic about creative activity, convinced of its benefits and able to maintain a positive attitude.

Creative activities are a likely resistance point for many people. Be prepared to hear, "I'm not creative" or "I can't draw." You may have to cajole reluctant participants—so think about ideas for dispelling anxiety and resistance, such as telling a funny story, showing one of your own (imperfect) creations, or giving people permission to use alternate methods, such as symbols, colors, and stick people instead of realistic drawings. Emphasize playfulness not performance.

Introduce provocative ideas, books, persons, objects, and procedures. Bring an old shoe and ask participants to create a metaphor for what the shoe represents in their own life. Encourage manipulation of ideas and objects. Novelty is stimulating, piques interest, and keeps people on their toes, especially if presented in a lighthearted, humorous way.

Decide whether creative activities are worth the time investment. Creative activities take time, so you need to ask yourself if the benefit is worth the time invested for your group, keeping in mind its purpose, setting, and schedule. If you decide to include creative activities, make a trial run to find out exactly how long an activity takes and then allow an extra five minutes to cover unexpected delays.

Creative activities can be chaotic or emotional. If you like control, be prepared to deal with your own anxiety. Rehearsal is helpful. Practice staying calm and focused during a whirlwind of creativity or emotion—like the eye of a storm. Remind yourself that tears are not lethal, and while some people may shed tears when sharing meaningful artwork, they quickly recover when their time in the spotlight is over.

Ambiguity and creativity go hand in hand. You need to give clear instructions, but don't give in to the temptation to overexplain. Let individuals who want a road map stew a little and make up their own minds about what to do.

Come prepared. Avoid last-minute scrambles by planning ahead. Make a list of the art supplies and equipment that are needed and pack generous amounts so there will be plenty for everyone, with some to spare. Visit the group room early and arrange the physical space into the type of work areas needed, making sure the space is equipped with facilities to handle the activities you have planned.

CAUTIONS

Plan for time to process feelings. Creative activities always arouse some emotion, and it's important to allow time to share feelings. In most cases, brief sharing will be enough, but with ongoing groups, it may take longer. Stick to time limits as much as possible, even when individuals display strong emotions and seem to want more time and attention. Offer to talk further with these individuals after the session, and keep things moving so everyone has a chance to be heard.

Avoid power struggles with highly resistant people. Enlist cooperation in some other way; for example, tell the person who says he can't write to draw a picture instead or describe his vision verbally to a partner. Ask skeptics to help distribute materials or work with a buddy on a selected task. Do whatever works and gets people involved.

Make sure the activity is safe for all. Ask about disabilities and make necessary adjustments. If the activity requires movement, can people in wheelchairs maneuver in the room? Can visually impaired people participate without getting hurt? Is the activity psychologically safe? Never intentionally embarrass or shame someone. It is sometimes tempting to put individuals or small groups on the spot—but don't do it, not even as a joke.

133 CARTOON CAPTIONS

Participants find humor in challenging situations by creating cartoons about current life stress or goals.

Goals

To find humor in a personal situation or dilemma.

To get acquainted in a lighthearted way.

Time

10–15 minutes

Materials Needed

Paper, colored markers, masking tape.

Process

1. Begin with a few open-ended questions about participants' motivations for attending the group. Solicit a few quick responses from four or five people.

   ■ What brought you here today?

   ■ What are you hoping to accomplish?

2. Summarize common motivations and comment on the benefits of a lighthearted approach to learning or problem–solving. Guide people in a reflection on the lighter side of their stressful situations or challenges.

   ■ Think about your personal reasons for coming today, including events or situations which may have stimulated you to come as well as motivations like hopes and dreams for change.

   ■ Now try to find some humor in your situation. If you were to portray your situation or motivations in a cartoon, how would you do it?

3. Distribute paper and colored markers and explain that participants will get acquainted by creating personal cartoons, which they will share with other group members. Encourage everyone to relax and have fun making something up.

- Write your first name in the upper right-hand corner of your paper.
- Now create a cartoon depicting your current situation, your feelings about being here, or your hopes and dreams for change.
- Your cartoon could be a dialogue or soliloquy.
- Feel free to draw in props or symbols as well as words.
- You have five minutes to create your own comic strip. Have fun with it.

4. When five minutes are up, divide large groups into groups of six, and when everyone is settled, give directions for introductions.

- Introduce yourself to the group, using your cartoons.
- Each person has two minutes to share.

Announce the time every two minutes.

5. When small-group sharing is done, ask participants if they would be willing to hang their cartoons in a gallery so others can read them during breaks. Provide masking tape and have people hang their cartoons in the designated space. Allow extra time for reading cartoons during breaks.

Variations

- Cartoon Captions would make an excellent closing exercise. Ask participants to write a dialogue summarizing the course or group experience. They should include their hopes at the beginning, key learnings, and plans for action.
- This exercise is easily adapted for other educational or therapeutic group purposes. For example, in parenting classes, have parents first draw a cartoon of a typical problem communication between themselves and their child. Then, as a closing exercise, have them draw a cartoon applying their newly learned parenting skills to this same situation.

CREATIVITY À LA CARTE

134 TIME/LIFE MAP

Materials: blank paper, markers or crayons

1. Think about your typical week, day, or month. Bring to mind all the things you do: your work, your play, your roles, and your responsibilities. Be aware of how much time and importance you give to each one.

2. Make a map or diagram of your life. Draw a large circle or other shape on the paper and divide the shape into sections which represent the aspects of your life that you visualized. Let each piece reflect the amount of time or importance you give to that aspect. Decorate with symbols, colors, images, words, and phrases. Label each section.

3. Study your map and reflect on your life patterns. Is there any aspect you want to change? Are there some parts you would like to see smaller or larger, added or eliminated?

4. Share maps with a partner or small group.

135 THINK BIG

Materials: blank paper

1. Do what you can to create a relaxed, lighthearted mood in group, setting the stage for creativity and humor.

2. Distribute paper and ask participants to write a funny memo suggesting a big idea to someone. The memo can be to anyone they choose, on any topic they want, real or fictitious. (If desired, memos can be focused on specific issues relevant to the group.)

3. Have individuals read their memos aloud to the entire group or share in small groups. Some ideas may be of value for realistic problem solving and planning. If you want, you can highlight these ideas for reference later on.

Variation: Before reading memos, have participants exchange papers and let someone else read their memo to the group.

©1998 Whole Person Associates 210 W Michigan Duluth MN 55802 (800) 247-6789

136 TANTRUMS

1. Have participants demonstrate, nonverbally, how they expressed anger at three different points in their lives: childhood, adolescence, and early adulthood.

2. Follow up with a discussion of commonalties discovered by the group and apply this to the learning goals of the group.

137 EXCLAMATIONS!

Worksheet: *Exclamations!* (page 145)

1. Ask participants to imagine what happens when stress accumulates to the point that they explode, outwardly or inwardly. What does this stress-mess look and sound like in mild, moderate, and big doses?

2. Distribute worksheets and ask people to draw or write descriptions for each type of stress-mess, starting with small splashes in the upper left corner, and moving clockwise around the sheet from moderate to big bursts. Describe each stress bubble with words, sentences, colors, and symbols depicting exclamations at each level of stress.

3. Share in pairs or small groups.

138 T-SHIRT BILLBOARD

Worksheet: *T-Shirt Billboard* (page 146)

Materials: colored markers or crayons

1. Give everyone a worksheet and drawing tools.

2. Invite individuals to make up a slogan about stress or wellness and write or draw the design on their T-shirt billboard.

3. Use the T-shirts for introductions and for sharing names, slogans, and learning interests.

4. Hang all billboards on a wall.

Variation: Adapt the slogan to another issue pertinent to your group and goals.

139 PREPOSITIONS

Worksheet: *Prepositions* (page 147)

1. Distribute worksheets and ask people to write a sentence about the day's topic for each preposition.

    ▨ Use the preposition in the sentence.

    ▨ Underline each preposition used.

    ▨ Do as many as you can in three minutes. You don't have to do them in order. If you can't think of something right away, move on to the next word.

    Give several examples (I'm buried *under* a ton of paperwork; I'm not sure *about* the new performance standards).

2. Invite people to share their experiences with a partner.

Variation: Choose a topic on which you'd especially like participants to expand their thinking. This icebreaker should generate lots of ideas.

140 B-ING STORY

Worksheet: *Story B* (page 148)

1. Give a brief introduction to the next agenda topic.

2. Distribute worksheets and invite participants to the story bee.

    ▨ Choose one list of five B-words.

    ▨ Write a brief story about (the selected topic), using all five words from the list at least once.

    ▨ When you finish, choose a second word list and write another B-story.

3. Invite participants to read their stories. Then use the stories as a springboard to further discussion.

141 CHARADES

Materials: In advance, prepare a set of "skill tags" (sticky labels or index cards with pins). Write on each tag a different skill that would be useful for the people in your group.

1. Divide the large group into two or more groups of six people.

2. Put a skill tag on the back of one person in each group.

3. In each group, the other people act out the skill like a charade, until the person with the label guesses what is on his back.

4. Repeat with a different skill and person in each group, continuing the game until each person has had a chance to guess a skill while others do the charades.

142 STATUES

1. Form groups of eight to ten people.
2. Make a group sculpture that depicts some aspect of the day's topic, positioning everyone in the group in symbolic body postures and movements.
3. Each group displays its statue art for the whole group, first silently, then with a brief explanation of its meaning.

143 BILLBOARD

Materials: paper, colored markers and string, paper punch available.

1. Distribute materials and provide instructions.
2. Make up a ludicrous ad on the group's topic and write it on your billboard, for example, Avoid Conflict with Effective Eyebrow Movements. Call 721-ARCH for help.
3. Fashion a bolo-tie tie name tag by punching holes in the top two corners, lacing a piece of string through, and tying a knot in back to create a necklace. Write your name in a corner, put it around your neck, and walk around the group. Introduce yourself to three people in three minutes, and share your ad.

144 BALLOON COLLAGE

Materials: seven-inch balloons, inflated and tied shut, for each participant, magazines, scissors, glue

1. Give each participant a balloon and make other materials easily accessible by all.
2. Cut out pictures and words from magazines and glue them to the balloon, covering the entire balloon with symbols of personal interests, values, hobbies, and philosophy of life.
3. Share balloon collages in small groups and then pin all to a wall.

Variation: Create subject collages, such as healthy life-style balloons.

145 TONGUE DEPRESSOR CONTRAPTIONS

Materials: twenty tongue depressors for each small group, quick-drying glue, a box of colored markers

1. Participants form small groups and work as a team of inventors or artists.

2. Using their supplies, each group creates an object, work of art, or product related to the group's topic. Allow five minutes for construction.

3. Each team shows its artistic contraption to the large group and then displays its invention on a table, where it will serve as an inspiration for all to continue to be creative.

146 PROBLEM PICTURE

Materials: blank paper, colored markers for all

1. Draw a picture of a current problem, using colored markers to highlight your design.

2. Introduce yourself by telling your first name, briefly explaining the meaning of your problem picture, and telling what you hope to learn in the group.

147 FEELING SKETCH

Materials: blank paper, colored markers for all

1. In three minutes, draw a picture or graphic design of your current mood, including your feelings about participating in this group. Use colored markers to depict different feelings and their intensity.

2. Take one minute to introduce yourself and tell about your feeling sketch.

148 CLAY SPIRIT

Materials: golf-ball size piece of clay for each participant

1. Use clay to shape an image representing your spirit. Let your imagination guide you in whatever direction it chooses. Allow your ideas to unfold freely and take shape in the clay. You have five minutes to mold your image.

2. Share in small groups.

149 PATCHWORK QUILT

Materials: a sheet of newsprint and colored markers or crayons for each person, masking tape

1. Invite participants to design a personal patchwork quilt.

   ■ Start with a first name patch that shows your name.

   ■ Then add other patches symbolizing important aspects of your life, such as your family, friends, work, church, and hobbies.

2. Allow five minutes for designing the quilts and then invite participants to share quilt stories with partners or in small groups.

3. Hang all quilts.

Exclamations!

T-Shirt Billboard

Prepositions (A-F)

About
_____

Above
_____

Across
_____

After
_____

Against
_____

Along
_____

Among
_____

Around
_____

At
_____

Before
_____

Behind
_____

Below
_____

Beneath
_____

Beside
_____

Between
_____

Beyond
_____

By
_____

Down
_____

During
_____

Except
_____

For
_____

Prepositions (F-W)

From
_____

In
_____

Inside
_____

Into
_____

Like
_____

Near
_____

Of
_____

Off
_____

Out
_____

Over
_____

Through
_____

To
_____

Toward
_____

Under
_____

Underneath
_____

Up
_____

Upon
_____

With
_____

Within
_____

Without
_____

Story B

Balance

Boredom

Beauty

Belief

Breakfast

Bearable

Become

Bitter

Better

Bizarre

Bouquet

Broadcast

Bridge

Brag

Business

Bond

Bind

Binge

Blink

Biology

Because

Beginning

Browse

Budget

Bulge

Birthday

Bicycle

Blame

Blah

Blink

Bonus

Bagel

Balloon

Burn

Back

_____

_____

_____

_____

_____

COMPLEMENTS & CONDIMENTS

Zesty Interludes

Sauces & Seasonings

ZESTY INTERLUDES

All groups need a periodic change of pace: breathing room or natural pauses that refresh, energize, and prepare people for a smooth transition to the next activity.

GROUP DYNAMICS PRINCIPLES

There is a natural ebb and flow in group process. There are energetic high points and also moments of lethargy or flagging energy and attention. This is not the leader's fault; it is inherent in group dynamics. Unfortunately, you can't always predict when it will happen. Be prepared to provide a mood-changing interlude when needed.

The leader needs to be skilled at recognizing the mood swings of a group. Leaders can't always predict the mood of the group, but they can listen to unspoken signals of fatigue, respect these feelings enough to allow breaks, and guide the group in a relaxing and refreshing activity. It's important to know how to turn down (or up) the intensity level, the play quotient, the feeling level, and the interpersonal involvement, so participants can sustain learning without becoming drained.

It's important to take time needed to help the group members change their mood. You, as the leader, have probably already shifted, but the collective mood shift takes intentional preparation and time for all to get on board.

Some groups will need physical energizers; others may just need a shift in mental focus or a brief relaxation break. If you've been doing most of the talking, an interpersonal energizer is likely to revitalize and reengage the group. Put yourself in the shoes of participants and imagine what you would want if you were in their place. Chances are you'll know intuitively what is needed to fill participants with new energy.

A general rule of thumb is to balance an activity with its opposite. Move after sitting; talk after being quiet; laugh after serious discussion; play after mental concentration. A change of activity converts lagging energy into electric energy.

Moods are contagious. One or two disgruntled, gloomy group members can dim the enthusiasm of other participants; while a few expansive, indefatigable participants can perk up the entire group. A leader with a sense of adventure and humor can transmit excitement and bend participants toward impressive, tireless efforts. Because moods are contagious, make yours positive and model this consistently for the group.

TIPS FOR PLANNING AND IMPLEMENTATION

Don't hurry. But don't ask the group if they're ready or what they need. Your job is to anticipate the need for mood change in advance—and then, in the present moment, choose from several alternatives the activity that best fits the situation.

Plan a sequence of activity that moves as fluidly and easily as possible. Move from heavy or serious content to a more lighthearted perspective, from fun and games to introspection and problem-solving, from low-risk sharing to more intimate self-disclosure. When activities are organized thoughtfully, change is gradual, and participants are induced to try new things without becoming pensive, rebellious, or shocked.

Always tie an energizer activity to the content you are covering or the group process. After a tense or emotion-laden exchange, have everyone take a deep-breathing break. Explain the connection, so people understand why you have chosen this activity. Connecting energizers to previous activities is one way to make transitions go smoothly and make sense to participants.

Pay attention to nonverbal cues. When people start yawning, rubbing their eyes, looking out the window, squirming in their seats, or looking at the clock—you know it's time for a break or change of activity.

Introduce and lead energizers with confidence and enthusiasm. The leader's attitude is contagious. Why should people get excited if you aren't? How can people feel comfortable when you're obviously ill at ease? Plan activities you sincerely enjoy and feel confident doing. If you're nervous about trying something new or different, rehearse it beforehand.

Physical environment affects mood and energy. Make the environment as ideal as possible with moderate temperature, good (not harsh) lighting, comfortable chairs, nourishing snacks, and other physical amenities that will enhance the group's mood and energy.

Change membership in small groups for energizers. Participants who have worked diligently with one group might play frivolously with another. Different people evoke different responses, so mix up the group now and then and watch people be jolted from a dulled mood into an expectant one.

CAUTIONS

Don't force your preplanned agenda if a mood change isn't needed. Don't use energizers at random or on schedule—save them for when your group (and you) need them most.

It takes some people longer than others to shift gears. Anticipate this and expect some resistance when you change activities. Don't let moans and groans put you off, but recognize that some individuals need more time and space for plugging into the new routine.

Don't overexplain. Subtlety is desirable whenever possible.

Don't wait too long. If you delay until people are overwhelmed by serious discussion or conflictual interaction or bored by irrelevant processes, it's much more difficult to change the mood.

Be cautious about energizers involving physical contact between participants. Most groups with more than a dozen participants will include someone who has been a victim of physical or sexual abuse. Touch, however gentle and friendly, can be traumatic for some individuals. Always provide an alternative way for people to participate without touching, and give people choices, such as a group back rub or a self-administered neck massage, so people who choose to not touch can do so without sacrificing participation or losing face.

150 MULBERRY BUSH

Participants experiment with different speeds of walking and talking, discover their natural rhythm, and explore the need for a change of pace.

Goals

To provide a welcome change of pace.

To identify personal, natural rhythm of walking and talking.

Time

5–10 minutes

Process

1. Clear the room of chairs and other furniture so there is plenty of space for participants to move freely in a large circle and then guide participants through a series of tempos as they walk around the circle. Vary the speed from very, very slow to very, very fast.

   ■ Walk around the circle at a casual pace and notice how you feel as you walk.

   ■ Now speed up your tempo. Walk faster and faster until you are walking at a speed much faster than your normal pace.

   ■ How do you feel now? What happens when you walk this fast?

   ■ Now return to your normal, natural rhythm. Walk around the circle the way you usually move and notice how you feel.

   ■ Try slowing your movements to a snail's pace. How does this feel?

2. Pause briefly to allow personal sharing about this experience.

   ■ Pair up with a neighbor and take one minute each to share what it felt like to move slower, faster, and at your normal pace?

   ■ Talk about the pace of group activity today and how you

feel about it. Is it too fast, too slow, or just right for you?

3. Survey the group to see how many participants feel the pace is too fast, too slow, or just right. Then instruct each pair to join another pair.

   ■ Ask another twosome to join you, to make a group of four, and sit down together.

4. When everyone is settled in a small group, ask participants to experiment with the tempo of their conversation.

   ■ Go around the group and tell your first name, using your normal tempo of speech.

   ■ Now discuss the advantages and disadvantages of changing group activities or routines, talking as fast as you can for one minute.

5. Signal time to stop speeding and start crawling—in a new, slowed-down pace.

   ■ Continue to talk about the pros and cons of changing group activities or routines, this time talking as slowly as you can for one minute.

6. Interrupt a third time, and instruct participants to continue the conversation in their normal speed of talking.

   ■ Keep talking for one more minute, but return to your normal conversational speed.

7. Call a halt to conversational speed experiments and ask small groups to discuss their responses to varying speeds of talking.

   ■ Share your responses to talking in three speeds: fast, slow, and normal.

8. Invite volunteers to share discoveries about the effect of different speeds on their participation and learning. Summarize the need for a change of pace and introduce activities selected to meet this need, either speeding up, slowing down, or continuing at your previous pace.

©1998 Whole Person Associates 210 W Michigan Duluth MN 55802   (800) 247-6789

ZESTY INTERLUDES À LA CARTE

151 ME, MYSELF, AND I

1. After a period of industrious group activity, give participants time for peaceful, silent affirmation. Ask them to take a deep breath and release it slowly, close their eyes, continue breathing deeply and slowly, and take a minute to appreciate and affirm themselves for all the things they did to get to the group today and for the energy they've given so far.

2. After a minute of quiet reflection, ask participants to slowly open their eyes, stretch, and prepare to move on to the next activity.

152 WINDMILL

1. After an intense session or period of hard work, invite participants to release tension with this exercise.

   ■ Stand up straight with your arms out in front of you.

   ■ Inhale and hold a complete natural breath as you swing your arms backward in a circle several times then reverse directions.

   ■ Exhale forcefully through your mouth.

   ■ Repeat the purifying breath, rotating your arms alternately, like a windmill.

153 BODY SWING

1. Tell participants to squat on their haunches and swing their body and arms as far to the left and then to the right as they can. They should keep their head forward and inhale while swinging in one direction and then exhale while swinging the other way.

154 HEAD MASSAGE

1. After a period of intense concentration, ask participants to give themselves a head massage. Tell them to massage with circular motion, starting at their forehead and moving to their temples and around their ears to the back of their head.

2. When they return to their forehead, they should use all four fingers to plow a series of rows on their head, back to the base of the scalp. Then they should use their thumbs to massage the base of their skull from the center to underneath the ears and back to center.

3. Tell them to finish by lightly tapping the entire head area to stimulate the body and mind.

155 WHISPERS

Materials: blank paper

1. Tell participants to roll up a sheet of paper, creating a tube or speaking horn for whispering messages. Tell them to use the paper speaker to whisper some bad news about themselves to another group member. They should then find a new person and whisper some good news about themselves.

2. Ask everyone in the group to whisper all at once, to no one in particular, an affirmation about themselves, then whisper this affirmation into their own ear, using their paper tubes.

3. Encourage participants to whisper affirmations to themselves several times a day.

156 STRUT YOUR STUFF

Props: CD or cassette player and lively music

1. Ask everyone to stand up and imagine their body as perfect in every way—physically tuned, shaped, healthy, and beautiful. They should pretend that they are totally happy with the way they look and feel and imagine that life is as good as it can be.

2. Turn on the music and instruct participants to act as if they believe all these good things about themselves. Encourage them to walk around and strut their stuff. They should enjoy their walk and notice how they feel in all parts of their body as they walk around.

3. Give participants time to write reflections about how they felt about themselves during this walk and note any difference between this experience and their typical walk.

©1998 Whole Person Associates 210 W Michigan Duluth MN 55802   (800) 247-6789

157 DAYDREAMS

1. To restore energy and balance, try using a brief guided meditation. Ask participants to find a comfortable spot, get as relaxed as they can, and breathe deeply and slowly. Play soft instrumental music in the background as you read a guided meditation of your choosing.

Variation: Instead of using a script, invite participants to create their own relaxing (or energizing) daydream. Allow several minutes for mood changing. If desired, have people pair up and share their daydreams.

©1998 Whole Person Associates 210 W Michigan Duluth MN 55802   (800) 247-6789

SAUCES & SEASONINGS

It's the little things—jokes, laughter, games, music, props, drama, ceremony, and ritual—that when sprinkled throughout group activity, add just the right flavor of humor, intrigue, and tenderness to your group, blending good-natured fun with bold learning.

GROUP DYNAMICS PRINCIPLES

Increasing the play quotient reduces stress. Playful activity provides a break, engages people in nonlinear thinking and gives a sense of perspective. Laughter is healthy. It often follows tears, when in the depths of despair, the absurdity of the situation strikes us. It's an enormous relief to laugh at ourselves.

Shared laughter connects people. When group members laugh together, a feeling of camaraderie pervades the group. Our humanity is touched; common threads between people become visible, like forest spider webs glimpsed when the light is right.

Humor and play give the leader an opportunity to do something outrageous. A good leader has a bit of magic and knows when to laugh and play. A good leader can be farcical without being flippant, robust without being racy or bawdy, dramatic or theatrical without being phony. Infusing group activity with surprising twists and turns, salty words, subtle humor, and wholesome fun keeps the group lively, curious, and involved.

Props and paraphernalia are inexpensive, ready tools for imaginative play and learning. Even when you are dazzling or brilliant in your use of props, group members will surpass you. The beauty of using props or symbolic objects like paper cups or rubber gloves is that participants will invent new, unimagined uses for them, accentuating the process with their own brand of humor, informally harmonizing the group with flashes of comedy, infusing the group with laughter and good humor.

Magic and play stimulate creativity and learning. Adults need permission and structure for letting go of adult controls and inhibitions and becoming relaxed, carefree, curious, spontaneous, bold, alive, imaginative, wondering, intuitive, and childlike. Instead of diverting people from learning, boisterous play—carefully planned—

usually enhances it, enriching group activity with unstudied discovery.

Rituals and ceremonies infuse the group with meaning. Rituals and ceremonies are symbolic expressions of shared meaning, something all participants can do to celebrate, sanctify, or honor their experience together. A closing ritual of affirmation or symbolic gift-giving, for example, can provide comfort and closure. Such ceremonies can be tender and moving, touching people in surprisingly meaningful ways.

Rituals can be simple or complex. A simple ritual for introduction, such as "I'm Joe and I'm an alcoholic," is powerful. Besides giving structure and format at the awkward beginning of a group meeting, simple rituals provide continuity for ongoing groups, so everyone knows what to expect from week to week. Complex rituals, such as a three-step planning process or a five-step activity for summarizing learning and saying good-bye, are effective ways to magnify key points and affirm individual effort. Experiment with different types of rituals and notice the way they enhance group dynamics.

TIPS FOR PLANNING AND IMPLEMENTATION

There is an art to using humor. Whenever possible, engage the group in an activity (skits, pantomime, nonsense syllables or songs) that will stimulate their own creativity and evoke the playfulness within.

Use contextual humor, not canned. Funny stories, jokes, and other amusing antics should be done within the context of the group's culture, values, goals, purpose, and style. If you're leading a parenting group, tell funny stories about parenting; if you're teaching about stress, focus your wit on this theme. Canned humor is not only irrelevant, it turns people off.

For ideas about props and paraphernalia, visit a craft store. Browse for little things that symbolize a coping skill or attitude. For example, miniature red flags could be used as props for discussion about red flags for stress, rubber clown's noses for humor awards, marbles for crystal balls and problem-solving. Let your creativity flow from things you see and trust your intuition. Use free association to discover new ideas and applications and then integrate these ideas into your work. Props will spice up your presentations and add whimsy to group activities.

When using props and paraphernalia, organize materials carefully. Nothing is more stressful than frantically searching for a missing prop or supply while group members wait for you to get your act together. This happens to every group leader sometimes, but there's no reason for props to be a recurring nightmare. Make it a habit to keep a checklist of props and other supplies and use it regularly. Keep your props and paraphernalia well-arranged and in working order.

Anticipate transitions the group will experience during the group and create rituals to ease them through these turning points. Think of what you want the ritual to accomplish: affirm participants, energize people, change the mood, or provide closure. Then design rituals to satisfy these needs or purposes.

Match your rituals to the group. Secret handshakes or foolish antics may not appeal to corporate executives. But don't be afraid to indulge your creativity. Borrow rituals from anywhere: victory dance, the wave, high fives, Mr. Rogers, or the evening news. Borrow rituals from your participants' symbol system: corporate slogans, e-mail affirmations, or a football huddle. Or have the group members create their own rituals.

Often ideas for rituals emerge spontaneously from the group and its process. Be on the lookout for gestures, phrases, or interchanges you can transform into rituals.

CAUTIONS

When using props, keep it simple. Too much stuff is overwhelming for participants and group leaders.

Beware of humor that diminishes another person. Don't allow put-downs among group members. Encourage people to laugh at themselves not at others.

Sometimes play interludes can be disruptive to the group. Play may be an invitation for clowns to avoid dealing with serious issues. Plan carefully.

If the group isn't cohesive, rituals may be hollow. Beware of empty rituals—we all have too many of these.

For ongoing groups, rituals can outlive their purpose or meaning. Periodically discuss your rituals and update with new ideas. Seek a balance between continuity and change.

Don't force yourself to do something that is not you. Every group leader has a unique style or personality. Successful group leaders do things that fit their style or personality; while unsuccessful group leaders fail to win the confidence of the group because they try too hard to do things they are not comfortable doing or to be something they are not. It's important to use humor, play, props, and rituals that you are comfortable with, so you can be authentic, relaxed, and enthused about what you are doing.

©1998 Whole Person Associates 210 W Michigan Duluth MN 55802   (800) 247-6789

ICEBREAKERS WITH PIZZAZZ

We hope that most of the activities in this book incorporate creativity and provide a bit of seasoning to spice up your workshop, presentation, or group meeting. If you are looking particularly for activities using props, rituals, humor, or a magic wand, consult the lists below for titles and page numbers.

Props and Paraphernalia

Many of the icebreakers in this book use props or other paraphernalia to make a point, to activate the group, to provide humor, or to stimulate creativity. Although such activities take some advance planning to have the designated item at hand, the impact is usually worth the effort.

Rubber Gloves 42   Megaphone 42
Monkey Wrenches 11   Picture Postcards 120
Hourglass 10   Contraptions 143
Flea Market 127   Baby Face 11
Greeting Cards 176   Group Quilt 70
Can of Squirms 117   Play Ball 114
Whole-Person Pacifier 96

For some icebreakers, the object or prop suggested could easily be developed into a worksheet, using clip art. On the other hand, real props could be substituted for worksheets with images. For example, the icebreaker *Pacifiers* could use a worksheet with a picture of a pacifier or a real pacifier as a prop.

Magic and Play

There are plenty of ideas for engaging participants in childlike play, fantasy, and imaginative, creative activity:

Superstar 14   Exaggeration 7
Fun and Games 8   Unbelievable Me 7
Baby Face 11   Walk In My Shoes 8
Mystery Guest 9   Treasure Hunt 67
What's My Line? 13   Dozen Gifts 37
Megaphone 42   Body Conversation 70
Moving Questions 70   Star Trek 83
Fairy Tales 83   Bingo 84

Rituals

See the chapter Dessert: Farewells & Resolutions for a variety
of ideas for closing rituals:

Exercises involving rituals are sprinkled liberally throughout
the book and found in all chapters:

DESSERT

Farewells & Resolutions

FAREWELLS & RESOLUTIONS

Not only do participants need the opportunity to consider, make, and publicly affirm insights and resolutions from the learning experience, they need to say good-bye to the people who shared these experiences. Although we rarely think about the need for icebreakers to help people engage with each other in their declarations of learning and desired change and in their expressions of farewell, they provide structure for easing people through these important closing rituals.

GROUP DYNAMICS PRINCIPLES

People need closure; groups need closure. In our effort to complete the explicit and implicit agenda of groups, classes, and workshops, we often run out of time and don't provide the opportunity for participants to talk about what they have learned, how they intend to apply their learning, and what the experience—including relationships with other group members—has meant to them. People expect endings: like the last chapter of a good book or a period at the end of a sentence—the group is not complete without one.

Termination is the final stage of a group's development. Just as getting acquainted, building trust, and setting the agenda are impor-tant for early stages of group development, wrapping up, evaluation, planning, saying good-bye, and letting go are vital for the final stage. Some attention to these issues, however brief, will give participants a process for moving gracefully through this stage.

Many people need a structured process for synthesizing learning and planning for implementation. Inner-focused individuals, espe-cially, need processing time to articulate their insights. They are unlikely to volunteer resolutions without some sort of group process that involves everyone.

Speaking aloud provides a powerful witness to resolutions. When participants proclaim their goals publicly, they are more likely to adhere to them. Public testimonials not only bolster motivation for change, they provide an opportunity for participants to receive needed support and encouragement from other participants.

Listening to insights and resolutions gives the leader concrete feedback. As a leader, you need feedback from participants to evaluate your own effectiveness with the group and to make refinements that keep your work polished and powerful.

For longer groups, especially, people will have feelings about the group ending. There may be sadness, fear, relief, hope, excitement, fatigue, and other feelings as participants prepare to leave, especially if they have invested considerable time and energy in the group. Providing a structure for expressing these feelings, while at the same time disengaging from the group, is one way to demonstrate sensitivity for group members and reinforce an important self-care skill: attending to feelings.

The length, depth, and intensity of your farewell process should match the investment participants have made. For a one-shot presentation, brief farewells in small groups or an invitation to remain and talk informally may suffice. A day-long workshop deserves a more extended opportunity for saying good-bye to people met during the day. For an extended learning experience, provide a structure for direct, positive feedback or gift-giving among participants.

Saying good-bye teaches skills for letting go. Many people have difficulty saying good-bye or letting go; we don't like the pain of separation and loss, and we feel awkward expressing feelings of affection, gratitude, and grief about leaving new friends or a supportive group. Saying farewell in a group gives us an opportunity to practice skills that can be immediately applied to daily life, because we all experience separations from people we care about or who have been important to us.

TIPS FOR PLANNING AND IMPLEMENTATION

Protect time for processing and sharing resolutions. As tempting as it may be to sacrifice this time for other items on the agenda, don't do it—people need time for intentional, unhurried processing and for sharing resolutions.

If possible, tie the icebreaker activity that facilitates closure to the initial icebreaker in which people announced their goals. For example, use before-and-after letters, telegrams, sentence stems, and other formats that can be repeated.

If time is short, use partners or trios for sharing. Then ask if anyone needs or wants to publicly affirm their resolution to all present.

Be sure to share the insights you gathered from the group and at least one resolution for yourself. Besides modeling openness to learning, this shows everyone that you are human, not perfect, and that you can benefit from applying ideas and skills to your own life, just as participants can.

In an ongoing group, you may need time at the end of meetings to bid farewell to group members who are participating in their final session. Farewell rituals that you do every time someone leaves the group provide continuity and closure for all participants, not just the person leaving.

The final meeting of a general-session group may focus almost entirely on a recap of the experience, resolutions for the future, and some type of farewell ritual. This is a complete package for wrapping up and is most likely to satisfy participants as they conclude their group experience.

Guide participants in formulating specific, concrete, and realistic resolutions and plans. Choose activities or icebreakers that help participants focus on exactly what they want to do and when and how they'll do it. The more specific and realistic they can be, the better their chances of achieving these goals.

CAUTIONS

Be prepared for folks who are unwilling to acknowledge any resolutions for change. Encourage them to affirm what they hope to continue that is working well.

Watch out for phoniness. Do not force groups that have not developed a strong cohesiveness to engage in long, insincere good-byes.

Some people find endings especially difficult. For some people, the group ending may provoke a personal crisis in which they feel overwhelmed, abandoned, or panicked by the reality of facing difficult situations alone, without the support of the group. In anticipation of this possibility, come prepared with information about local resources and referral sources. Also, tell people you will remain after the group ends in case someone has questions or concerns they want to talk with you about privately.

158 PRESS RELEASE

Participants pair up with other group members, interview each other, write press releases, and read them aloud to the entire group, highlighting each person's learning and the application of that learning to real life.

Goals

To summarize learning and apply it to real life.

To affirm and support individual goals.

Time

10–15 minutes

Materials

Press Release worksheets (page 179)

Process

1. Start with a definition of a press release: a short, summary statement, written and usually read aloud by press secretaries or public relations staff, describing actions or responses of a public official to a specific event or issue, making this information public by releasing it to the media for publication or broadcast.

2. Hand out worksheets and explain that press releases usually include the type of information listed on the worksheet. Explain that as part of a final summary of their experience in the workshop, participants will interview each other and write press releases that can be read to the entire group. Provide the following instructions:

   ▪ Pair up with another group member and find a place where you can sit down together and talk with some privacy.

   ▪ First, decide who will be Press Secretary and who will be Elected Official. Elected Officials will be interviewed by Press Secretaries, who will ask the questions written on the Press Release and fill in the blanks on the form with key information obtained from Elected Officials.

■ This information will be released to the entire group, so Elected Officials should choose what they want to share publicly about what they learned in the group.

■ When Elected Official's Press Release has been written, switch roles, Elected Officials now interviewing Press Secretaries and filling out their Press Release.

■ You have about seven minutes to interview each other and write two press releases to share with the entire group.

4. When the allotted time has elapsed, reassemble the large group and ask a volunteer to start by reading a press release. Thank the volunteer and continue to have participants read press releases until each person's press release has been read.

■ For larger groups, tell each pair to join with three other pairs, forming groups of eight, and read press releases to each other.

Variation

Pair this closing exercise with a Press Release at the beginning of the session, which can be used to get acquainted and share reasons for coming to the group.

FAREWELLS & RESOLUTIONS À LA CARTE

159 THOUGHT SUBSTITUTES

1. As part of a final plan for change, have participants write down three negative things they usually say to themselves followed by three positive statements to replace the negative ones.

2. Ask participants to select one thought substitute to share with the large group and then have them take turns standing and reading positive and negative statements.

3. Assign homework.

   ▪ Repeat the positive statements aloud three times a day, every day for a month, until they become natural substitutes for your original negative thoughts.

160 RECYCLING PROGRAM

Worksheet: *Recycling Program* (page 180)

1. Hand out worksheets and invite participants to plan a process for transformation. They should list outdated attitudes that need revision, feelings that should be recycled, and other trash in their lives that needs to be creatively transformed into something good.

2. Allow participants to create their own unique recycling program, writing or drawing ideas on their worksheets under the steps to transformation.

3. Form small groups and ask members to take turns sharing their recycling programs by telling about their plans for change.

161 UNLEARNING

1. As part of a closing ceremony, have participants join a small group and take turns telling what they have unlearned or realized they need to unlearn as a result of the course or workshop.

2. Solicit examples of unlearning tasks participants have recognized during the workshop and summarize the relationship between unlearning and learning.

162 FIVE STEPS TO CHANGE

Worksheet: *Five Steps to Change* (page 181)

1. Give each person a worksheet. Guide participants through reflections about each step of the change process, instructing them to write specific ideas for each of the five steps on their worksheet:

   ▪ What have you decided to change?

   ▪ What is your plan for change?

   ▪ How and when will you put their plan into action?

   ▪ How and when will you evaluate your plan?

   ▪ How will you maintain change?

2. Ask participants to pair up with another group member and take turns sharing their five steps to change, incorporating suggestions partners may have for making the plan more specific or realistic.

163 LAST WILL AND TESTAMENT

Worksheet: *Last Will and Testament* (page 182)

1. Ask participants to rejoin their small groups and make a last will and testament. Distribute worksheets and guide people through the process, giving several examples at each point.

   ▪ Fill in your name.

   ▪ Give specific examples of healthy qualities of mind and body.

   ▪ Decide on something symbolic or realistic you would like to bequeath to the group as a whole, such as a joke, blessing, note, humor, or energy.

164 AUTOGRAPH PIE

Worksheet: *Autograph Pie* (page 183)

1. Tell participants to rejoin their small groups. Distribute worksheets and ask people to write their name on it and then pass it to the person on their left, who autographs a slice with their name and a note of remembrance, then passes it to the

next person, and so on around the group, until every person has autographed a slice of every other group member's pie.

2. Go around the group a second time, offering each person a chance to share autographed messages from other group members.

Variation: Hand out a second pie worksheet. Ask participants to divide it into slices according to the content of the session, write a question in each slice, and then discuss the questions in small groups or with the large group.

165 BLESSINGS

1. Divide into small groups and assign groups the task of making up a unique blessing to read to the group as a way as parting and saying good-bye. These can be prayers, poems, or simple statements focused on the topic of the day. To stimulate creativity, write an example, such as the Irish Blessing or a Biblical blessing, on the board.

2. Each group appoints a representative to stand up and read their blessing to the entire group. Thank each group for their blessing, and conclude by reading your own blessing (prepared in advance) for participants.

166 CLOSING STATEMENTS

Worksheet: *Closing Statements* (page 184)

1. Distribute worksheets, and invite participants to think back over the learning experience and respond to each statement.

2. When nearly everyone is finished, invite people to take turns reading one of their completed statements to the group.

2. If time remains, open the floor to further sharing of closing statements, before dismissing the group.

167 TEAM MESSAGE

Worksheet: *Team Message* (page 185)

1. Distribute worksheets and give instructions for capturing team messages.

■ Write your name at the top.

■ Pass your message sheet around the group.

■ Each person should choose a character and beside that character's letter write a message of affirmation or encouragement to the person whose name is on top

■ Each person should receive an affirming message from every other group member.

2. Go around the group, asking each person to share one message of affirmation or encouragement from their Team Message worksheet.

168 POINTERS

Worksheet: *Pointers* (page 186)

1. Hand out worksheets. Ask participants to recall pointers from today's course or workshop, making a list of key points on their worksheet.

2. Have people get into small groups and share pointers, taking a few minutes to pool wisdom and noting additional pointers from other participants.

3. Ask volunteers to share examples of pointers from the group, and summarize key ideas.

169 GREETING CARDS

1. Distribute inexpensive or computer-generated greeting cards (thank you, valentine, sympathy, friendship, blank, etc.). Ask each group member to choose a card for each individual in the group and write a greeting that celebrates something they like about that person.

2. When cards are completed, everyone distributes their greetings and reads those they receive.

Variation: Tailor the messages to your closing goals (e.g., a piece of advice, a memorable moment, a gift received from the other person, etc.).

170 WEEK AHEAD

1. Ask participants to pair up with another person, and tell one thing they are looking forward to in the week ahead.
2. Ask volunteers to share what they are looking forward to in the week ahead and then dismiss the group with encouragement to enjoy the things they are looking forward to that week.

171 SIGNPOST

Worksheet: *Signpost* (page 187)

1. Distribute worksheets and invite participants to summarize learning from the day, group, or course by making a variety of signs to advertise key insights and give direction to the road ahead.
2. Ask participants to read their signposts aloud in small groups. Then ask for volunteers to share examples of signposts with the entire group.

172 MAGIC PRESENT

Props: empty unwrapped box for each group

1. Have participants join their small groups and give someone in each group a box. Provide instructions on receiving symbolic gifts.

■ Imagine the box contains a magic present for you. What do you wish for inside the box? (Give some examples that fit the tone and issues dealt with by the group.)

■ Take a minute to describe your desired gift and how you might use it.

■ Then pass the box to your right so the next person can make a wish.

2. Instruct participants to pass the box around the group a second time, this time having one person hold it, while every other group member gives a symbolic magic present to that person (e.g., peace of mind, Nobel Prize for best discovery, solution to a problem).

173 PEACE PIPE

Worksheet: *Peace Pipe* (page 188)

1. Distribute worksheets and ask participants to reflect on the process of making peace.

    ■ Who do you need to make peace with?

    ■ How would you do it?

    ■ How willing are you to make peace?

    ■ What's the first step you will take today to make peace with this person?

2. Tell participants to pair up with someone and share their plans for peacemaking.

3. Invite volunteers to share how they are going to make peace with someone. Ask them to include the actions they are planning to take today. Offer support and encouragement, as well as cautions against inappropriate or aggressive confrontations with friends, family, or coworkers.

©1998 Whole Person Associates 210 W Michigan Duluth MN 55802   (800) 247-6789

Press Release

Date _____

FOR IMMEDIATE RELEASE

_____ recently completed
             (your name)

_____
    (group, workshop, or course name)

because of the following areas of concern:

_____

_____

Strategies discovered and rediscovered today were:

_____

_____

Immediate applications for real life that were made today are:

_____

_____

Recommendations include:

_____

Recycling Program

Outdated, bad attitudes that need revision:

Feelings that need to be recycled:

"Trash of my life":

Steps to Transformation

5 Steps to Change

1   What do I want to change?

2   What is my plan for change?

3   How and when will I put my plan into action?

4   How and when will I evaluate my plan?

5   How will I maintain this positive change?

Last Will and Testament

I, _____

being of sound mind and body, specifically
possessing these healthy qualities of MIND:

_____

_____

_____

and of BODY

_____

_____

_____

Do now bequeath

_____

_____

_____

to the group as a whole.

_____

Autograph Pie

Name: _____

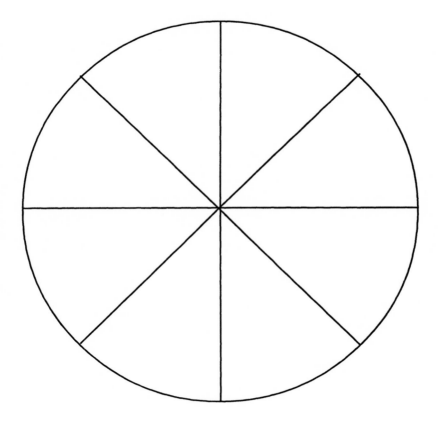

Closing Statements

I learned that _____

_____

I rediscovered that _____

_____

I changed my mind about _____

_____

I realized that I _____

_____

I had the most difficulty with _____

_____

The high point for me was _____

_____

I especially want to remember _____

_____

I am looking forward to _____

_____

I am determined to _____

_____

As a result of this experience, I _____

_____

POINTERS

Signpost

Peace Pipe

Who do I need to make peace with?

How would I do that?

How willing am I?

I'll take this first step today:

About Whole Person Associates

Whole Person Associates provides stress management, wellness promotion, and workplace productivity materials that actively involve participants and offer a "whole person" focus on body, mind, spirit, relationships, and lifestyle.

Counselors, trainers, therapists, educators, consultants, and group leaders use our resources, which include:

> Books of structured exercises on many topics, which are adaptable to different issues, age groups, learning styles, and life experiences
>
> Video courses on stress, healthy living, and workplace relationships
>
> Relaxation audio and video
>
> Self-help books
>
> Biofeedback equipment and popular Biodots
>
> Health promotion materials
>
> Resources for parents and teachers
>
> Ready-to-Run workshops
>
> Assessment tools

Call 800-247-6789 to request a catalog, or view or products and order online at www.wholeperson.com.

CPSIA information can be obtained at www.ICGtesting.com
Printed in the USA
BVOW022056110313

315264BV00003B/440/A

9 781570 252136